Start with
Hello

Start with Hello

How to convert today's stranger into tomorrow's client

LINDA COLES

WILEY

First published in 2013 by John Wiley & Sons Australia, Ltd
42 McDougall St, Milton Qld 4064

Office also in Melbourne

Typeset in 11/13.5 pt ITC Berkeley Oldstyle Std

© Blue Banana 20 Ltd

The moral rights of the author have been asserted

National Library of Australia Cataloguing-in-Publication data:

Author:	Coles, Linda
Title:	Start with hello: how to convert today's stranger into tomorrow's client / Linda Coles.
ISBN:	9780730304784 (pbk)
	9780730304791 (ebook)
Notes:	Includes index.
Subjects:	Public relations.
	Business networks.
	Social networks.
	Interpersonal relations.
	Interpersonal communication.
Dewey Number:	650.13

Cover design by Paul McCarthy

Cover image created by Wiley

Printed in Singapore by C.O.S. Printers Pte Ltd

10 9 8 7 6 5 4 3 2 1

Disclaimer

This book is dedicated to my hubby Paul, who is my constant source of inspiration.

Contents

About the author

 Hello! I'm Linda Coles, an international speaker and author with short spiky hair. I run a small company called Blue Banana and mainly work from my home office on a fig orchard in New Zealand. Paul is the love of my life, Stella and Monkey are my two cats and Daisy and Molly are my two goats.

My background is mainly in retail management working in some of the UK's biggest retailers, but life in the slower lane beckoned and so Paul and I moved to green pastures south of Auckland. The slower life never really happened, and I continue to work with some really great brands by helping them to build relationships with their customers online.

I speak a great deal and write about building relationships, an important part of being successful in business, and I wrote the book *Learn Marketing with Social Media in 7 Days* in 2011. I also write regularly as one of only 220 LinkedIn influencers, along with Richard Branson, Barack Obama and Arianna Huffington, which sounds very grand and I am very honoured to have been asked.

Mark Twain once said 'The two most important days in your life are the day you are born and the day you find out why'. And Albert Einstein said 'I fear the day that technology will surpass our human interaction. The world will have a generation of idiots'. I guess I have made it my purpose, my 'find out why', to keep people talking to each other, to help them become less focused on their smart phone and more interested in what and who is around them at any given time.

This book is very practical and very easy to read. My goal is to make this book accessible to everyone and so you don't need an MBA to be able to understand the concepts and the ideas. Above all, I want you to finish it, use the information, then pass it on to someone else, maybe a stranger, someone you don't know yet.

Feel free to look me up and say hello.

Facebook bluebanana20

LinkedIn bluebanana20

Twitter bluebanana20

Website bluebanana20.com

Email linda@lindacoles.com

Acknowledgements

My inspiration has come from many people and places, and I would like to say thanks. Thanks to everyone who submitted their stories and there are many of you. To Seth Godin for your daily inspiration, to Dave Kerpen for stretching my ideas, probably without even knowing it, to all of those people who have followed, connected and friended me adding more ideas into the pot, and to the great Team Wiley who have a knack for making a book a billion times better than the original raw manuscript.

Introduction

Let me start with hello.

Businesspeople all over the world are looking for new and alternative ways to market themselves and their businesses. By going back to good old-fashioned small talk and saying hello to strangers, more business opportunities and business connections will arise. People buy from people they know, like and trust, so get to know more people!

Talking to strangers does not come naturally to everyone. That's where this book can help. It guides you through the key skills you need to learn to start building effective relationships.

This book is for anyone wanting to:

- build business and social connections today and in the future
- meet more people but find it hard to start a conversation with someone they haven't met before
- be inspired with real-life examples of others who have taken the plunge by simply saying hello to a stranger
- mix up their daily schedule a bit to see where a little serendipity takes them.

By developing the art of saying hello to someone you don't know and starting a brief conversation you will be able to develop productive, profitable business relationships easily.

Peppered with real-life stories of how chance conversations have led to business relationships and new opportunities,

Start with Hello will show you how valuable a chance conversation can be—and how lucrative the return on investment (ROI) can be.

Divided into five parts, *Start with Hello* offers productive, creative ideas on:

- why we have historically had an aversion to talking to strangers and some easy ways of overcoming this and starting to engage and communicate with strangers

- the practicalities of networking with others, how to start a conversation and some freestyle networking ideas

- how to network effectively online using the most popular social networking sites and services

- how to develop a strategy for successfully connecting with new people and how to determine what sort of person you are talking to, using behavioural profiles

- how to use the art of chat to connect with people and build personal relationships—because chance meetings are not limited only to business.

By the time you have finished reading this book, you will be filled with the confidence to make the first move and to start a credible conversation with someone you don't know yet.

So start with hello, and convert today's strangers into tomorrow's clients.

Opening story

I picked this story about Erwin to begin this book because it is such a good example of someone saying hello resulting in something great happening. Why, saying hello to a stranger and sharing a drink in a bar not only earned him a substantial fee on a project, but it was also a turning point in his life. How proud Erwin must feel when he passes The Hague and sees the fruits of his labour displayed there for many thousands of others to enjoy too!

La fleur qui marche

I was a member of the Industrial Club in Amsterdam, a business club with more than 1600 members. One evening I started chatting with a man at the bar and he asked me what I did for a living. I had just been made redundant after a global reorganisation so I told him, 'I can sell everything you want me to sell.' To make a long story short, he introduced me to his wife, who owned a gallery and had a piece of art to sell that wouldn't move.

A couple of days later I met her and the art piece turned out to be a very large sculpture of the late Fernand Léger called *La fleur qui marche* (The walking flower). It was in crates and had been stored in Geneva for the past four years after being exhibited and owned by the well-known Rockefeller Foundation in New York. That Thursday morning I signed a contract with her and when I drove back I asked myself, 'How on earth am I going to do this?'

When I got back home, I was sitting in my study and all of a sudden my eye caught sight of a magazine called *Quote 500*, the Dutch rich list similar to the *Fortune* 500 list, and I thought, 'Hey, these people must have money to buy a million-dollar piece of art.'

I started reading from the first billionaire down to number 25 on the list and soon had a picture of people interested in collecting art. Then I asked myself, 'Who has the space?' The list of 25 became a short list of 10. The next challenge for me was getting in touch with them. After an internet search I found the first one. Having never sold art before, I didn't have a clue how to approach them but managed to get in touch with the personal assistant of my prospect, who asked, 'Can you fax it to me, so I can show him?' Was it that simple? I spent the rest of the day searching for the contact details of some of the others to call on Monday.

Monday afternoon I contacted the personal assistant of Joop van den Ende (co-founder of Endemol, a large media group estimated to be worth 1.6 billion euros at the time) and asked her if I could send details about the sculpture to him. The next day I got a call from him personally saying he was interested but at a lower price. That same evening I got back in touch with the owner to talk about the price and a counteroffer was made. On Wednesday Joop van den Ende got back to me and we met each other halfway on the price—a deal that had appeared to be impossible was done in less than a week.

I got my fee as soon as the transaction was done and the sculpture went on display next to Joop van den Ende's new theatre in the sea town of Scheveningen, next to The Hague, where it still features today. When you search on the internet you find a lot of photos of tourists standing next to the walking flower and to be honest, that makes me kind of proud.

This all happened with a drink, talking to a stranger, loving a challenge and thinking out of the box. It was a turning point in my career.

Erwin Versleijen

Part I

Why communicating with strangers is the key to business success

Meeting someone new can be called luck, fate, serendipity — or in some cases plain old bad luck — but either way, you have both found yourselves in the same place, or doing the same activity at the same time, allowing you to connect in some way. Something, somewhere has lined up the variables to make a connection happen, no matter how obvious or subtle.

Read the following chapters to learn how to:

- put yourself in situations where you can meet people
- take action to increase your opportunities for making business connections
- discover ways of finding common ground with strangers to build new relationships
- behave to ensure you engage successfully with people
- mix things up a little to increase your chances of stumbling across someone or something new and exciting.

Chapter 1

Is the internet limiting serendipity?

A stranger is simply someone you have not met yet.

Anon

Before computers there were many opportunities to meet people and have chance conversations that could lead to unexpected pleasant surprises. Long before we had email, we may have met someone we knew on our way to post a letter, or we may have bumped into someone new on our way to use the photocopier at the library. These chance encounters could be useful as well as quite pleasant. Another name for this is serendipity, meaning a 'happy accident' or 'pleasant surprise'—but for these opportunities to happen, we must first be alert to the possibility of them happening.

Stranger danger

'Never talk to strangers.' That's what your parents told you, didn't they? From a very early age, it has been ingrained into our culture that anyone we don't know is a stranger, and we should steer well clear of them. No eye contact, no smile, no form of acknowledgement whatsoever—zilch.

But what does this do to our ability to connect with other people and start an easy conversation later on in life?

It certainly makes it much harder for us to communicate with others, particularly in business situations. We may become wary, shy even, maybe feel a little uncomfortable or come across as immature because we simply haven't had enough practice at talking to people we don't know. If we have been told all our lives to keep away from strangers, why should we suddenly expect to be able to change at the drop of a hat or be able to interact easily with them just because we're in business?

It's even more apparent when we meet someone who is higher up the 'food chain' than we are: the chairman of a well-known company, a famous thought leader such as Deepak Chopra, a well-known business entrepreneur such as Richard Branson and others of a similar ilk. They are all human, they all started out at the bottom, they are all like us in many ways, and yet they appear so high up and out of our reach to talk to.

But there are easy ways to start conversations with such people. You just need to know the best way to attract their attention and take action. (All of this will be covered in parts II and III of this book.)

When we started out as children going off to kindy with our packed lunch and big smile, we had very little awareness about how to behave or what good manners were. We learned how to socialise over time, using the skills taught to us. Social rules are ingrained into our culture from somewhere way back in time when someone or a group of people decided what was right and what was wrong. Like any culture or religion, the unwritten rules have been handed down through the generations, and so it came to pass that our society too has rules that we 'must' adhere to in order to fit in and be 'normal'.

So, as children, when someone came to visit, we would become shy because we were only used to chatting with our parents or the adults we met at kindy. We would hide behind Dad's legs and keep quiet…Hardly the best start to becoming a confident young child.

Now I'm not advocating putting young people in harm's way, but simply pointing out the lessons that have been instilled into us over the centuries about not talking to strangers. In fact, we now know that most commonly when children are abducted or harmed it is not the work of strangers, but in fact someone the child is familiar with or even related to.

In reality, we don't grow too much in confidence through our teen years either—certainly not in relation to talking to strangers or elders anyway—but with people our own age, it's not such a problem.

Remember starting your first proper job as a young man or woman? How scary was your first day, your first week? No doubt you lacked confidence just like the rest of us, particularly when the boss came around.

I was just 16 when I got my first proper job in one of the most prestigious stores you could work in. Even though it was only part time, it was my foot in the door to get a better position as soon as it came up. The store boasted a very low staff turnover rate because they looked after their staff well. This meant that the staff were, on the whole, quite a bit older than I, many having worked at the store for decades. So how did I fit in: a young woman, lacking in confidence with my elders, with a complete lack of communication skills and work experience? It was tough. When the store manager, Mr Wood (you didn't use the store manager's first name back then) came onto the shop floor, I quaked in my boots, hoping he didn't ask me a question, particularly one I didn't know the answer to. But over time, I started to relax a little, get to know some of the older ladies and make some friends. It's around this time that you realise the only thing you have to offer until your communication skills mature is your personality, and you hope that shines through enough for you to make your mark.

I don't think my communication skills started to mature until I was in my twenties and was transferred to another store in another town where I had to adjust to another staff of older people. I ended up leaving after a short time and finding another job at a small chain store nearby.

Going through an interview process is a great way to work on your communication skills. You almost never have only one interview; there will be many, with different interviewers and first and second—and even third—interview processes. Putting yourself in an alien one-to-one position with a stranger, and talking about yourself and why you so desperately want the position on offer, can be a confidence builder if you work hard at it. If you can communicate, create a rapport with the interviewer and have the necessary skills to do the job, you stand as good a chance as the next person. No-one will employ a person they don't like or can't talk to, so if you are just starting out and feel you're lacking a little in confidence, work on your communication skills and creating a rapport. You will find more help with this in parts II and IV of this book.

Creating opportunities for serendipity

In order to come across serendipitous moments—or, simply put, stumble across something or someone new—we need to take some sort of action. But are we limiting the possibility of a knock-on effect taking place without even realising it? Prior to the electronic age, we had to physically search for and research everything we wanted or needed, which meant the opportunities for discovering new people and new facts were abundant. But is the new technology we're all in awe of a comparable alternative?

Searching for knowledge

Take learning for instance. Not so long ago, if we wanted to learn about a particular subject by researching it—say for a thesis or for writing a book—our options were pretty much limited to going to the library and finding what we needed. If you were lucky, the books you needed would be there and you could take them home for a week or two, at which time you would have to return them. If you were unlucky and the book you needed was out, you had to wait until it came back in or choose a different one. If it was a new book that you needed, there was always a waiting list. How inconvenient.

However, the act of going to the library made you more prone to having chance meetings of not only the human kind, but also with a piece of information that you weren't actually looking for. If the book you really wanted was in fact out, and you ambled along the shelves looking for alternatives, you may have found something even better than your original choice, or something with a different angle on the subject you sought, which in turn could well have led you down a very different path. Finding something more interesting than the intended, and quite by accident, can give you a quick zap of joy.

Another example of serendipity can be found in the daily newspaper (or, if you are like me, the weekend edition). I enjoy scanning the paper with a coffee on a Sunday morning in my chair in the sunny alcove of my house, but I don't only scan it. I look at the pictures and I read the headlines and if something grabs my attention, I'll read the whole article. What scanning does for me is it gives me the opportunity to find gems of stories that may interest me immediately, and it also gives me the opportunity to trigger something in my mind that says, 'Ah! Good idea' or 'Well I never knew that!' More importantly, I'm discovering great information by accident.

Here's a story about how Alice made what she found in the local free paper into a business.

Alice's story

When I was in San Diego for work I randomly came across an ad in the local free paper that said, 'Find us and we'll give you a free strand of lapis lazuli.' Now, as a child I had loved rocks and I attended geology lectures with one of my mother's friends when I was five years old. I just couldn't get enough of rocks and gemstones. I found the store, they gave me a free strand of lapiz and the rest is history.

I was so inspired by this that I decided to learn the techniques of making jewellery. I got to know the owner of the store, who used to own a gemstone-mining factory in Africa, and who has a team of artisans who manufacture products for QVC (a multinational corporation specialising in televised home shopping) and all of the big, upscale retailers in the US. He has connections around the world which I have taken advantage of to source precious and semiprecious stones. He is now my wholesaler for components. As a result of that ad I started a side business designing, making and selling one-of-a-kind jewellery to small upscale boutiques and private clients.

If she hadn't scanned the paper that day, Alice's stumble-upon moment would probably never have happened and she may never have found her side business opportunity.

But she did see the advertisement and she did take action and the end result was that she not only developed a keen interest in making and selling jewellery, but she developed a side business, a business that one day may become her full-time job. The return on investment (ROI) for Alice is a second income.

The information revolution

Unfortunately, acquiring information in the ways mentioned previously is a dying trend, a sign of the modern times, although we have found alternatives. But with these information areas going by the wayside, so too goes the chance of finding a serendipitous moment, or finding the unexpected. You may think that's not true; after all, we've got the internet, right? How much more information could you possibly need?

The internet does give things scale and speed, and you could say that a stumble-upon encounter has an even greater chance of happening because the internet is so vast. But we've become clever in the way we use it: we've learned how to refine searches!

We locate the 'search' function. We type in the keywords for the information we're looking for. And up pop possibly millions of pages of results. The search results are simply too big to deal with yet we know that what we're looking for could be on one of those many buried pages. But who carries on a search beyond the first two or three pages at best? We know we'll never see the rest of the search results because we're pretty much trained not to go past page three; that would be in the 'too hard basket' and time is always of the essence, so we move on and redefine our search.

You could argue that the answers we're looking for are right there on the first two or three pages and that we should scan the pages and find the answers, but in reality those first pages may throw up search results that are way too broad and useless. So we search again, this time narrowing our keywords down a little to make the results more targeted and closer to what we require. This will bring fewer results but they are likely to be more targeted to what we want, thus limiting our chances of serendipitous moments.

Music mania

Now let's take a look at what has happened to the way we discover and listen to music.

In the past we would have gone to record shops to find something in particular, such as a new album by our favourite artist, and browsed other categories while we were there. This increased our chance of finding something new and diverse that we had not set out to look for—it may have been the album that was being played at the time that we were in the store. The point is that we were being exposed to something new: new music by accident.

With iPods and smart phones holding all our music today, do you listen to the radio much any more, or do you only listen to what you have downloaded from iTunes or Spotify? We are very much in control of what we listen to, making sure we remove all of the sounds we don't want to hear, such as music we're not interested in and radio advertisements.

Many of us used to listen to the radio in the car, but again iPods have taken over and with the many podcasts that are now available, we even have a choice of not listening to music at all but to audio recordings or a conversation or presentation instead.

As a young girl, I spent my Sunday evenings locked away in my bedroom with the top 40 show on the radio and my trusty cassette tape recorder ready to make a copy of the show so that I could listen to it again and again. It was the highlight of the week music-wise. During the two-hour show I was exposed to punk, new wave, pop, classic, whatever was selling in the top 40, and I went out and bought a wide cross-section of music because of it. Today, however, falling over new sounds is becoming harder and harder, which is probably making it more difficult for new artists to become known.

e-Books

With the invention of electronic book readers such as the Kindle and the iPad, bookstores are in decline across the world and that means another place for serendipity to occur is slowly dying. From anywhere around the world, your book can be downloaded to your device within minutes with no delivery costs except for your data usage—and the book prices are much cheaper too. This has certainly made me read more books and in fact I don't buy books any other way now. If it's not on Kindle, I don't buy it.

These sorts of gadgets have the chance to revolutionise the way books are published and sold and they are doing just that. I can search for a book on my chosen online store, such as Amazon, read the reviews others have left of the book, click one button and, hey presto, it's arrived. When I have finished reading the book, it gives me a small selection of 'you might like this' books from which to choose my next book and again, because it is quick and cheap, I then purchase my next book right there and then with just one click, and without having to leave my Kindle.

This is both good and bad from a serendipity point of view because although I am exposed to another author who has a book similar to the one I have just finished, this method only gives me a very small sample of books to choose from. Whose books might I be missing out on? Or did I already have my serendipity moment when I acted on Kindle's suggestion of another book?

~

So many other areas of our lives have also been transformed by the electronic age we live in. Take for example the advent of magazine-style news websites such as www.mashable.com. With so much information available for free at our electronic fingertips, why pay to have it in hard copy form? But does this mean we will be left with fewer serendipitous moments?

Not necessarily. Consider how the way we share information with each other online can provide serendipitous moments. As you surf through your Facebook newsfeed, you can see what your friends are sharing with each other, often resulting in unexpected surprises or snippets of new information. Their comments too can provide you with interesting new information.

So the internet can be good for helping us find information and serendipitous moments. We just have to be aware and act on what we see to make them happen. Taking action is what we'll look at in the next chapter.

Chapter 2

Action brings activity

Action is the foundational key to all success.

Pablo Picasso

Sitting in your office, and particularly your home office, is not going to give you opportunities to say hello to someone you have never met before. To do that, you'll have to get out for at least a few minutes and go to, say, a coffee shop. So let's plan a few events to enter into your calendar and get the ball rolling in the right direction.

Being in a familiar environment but in an unfamiliar situation is one way of taking the pain out of pushing yourself to strike up a conversation with someone you don't know, as does having something in common. For example, if you're a regular at your local chamber of commerce networking events, this is a familiar environment to you but, as you don't know the other guests there yet, it is an unfamiliar situation.

The obvious first question you might ask another guest at such as an event would be, 'How long have you been a member?' Easy. You have something in common, and it enables you to break the ice, giving the other person an opportunity to start talking about themselves first—and most people love to talk about themselves!

If you have read Dale Carnegie's book *How to Win Friends and Influence People* you will know that one of his six principles for being a good listener is to get people talking about themselves. It's not unusual for people to like talking about themselves—most likely, much of the time they are probably not even aware that they are talking about themselves because they feel that they are simply taking part in a conversation with you and enjoying it.

Following up from that initial question, you might ask them about other events they have attended recently, or even move on to ask them what they do for a living, so that they can offer some more detail about themselves. Here's one way you could do this.

Try this

What can you pick out of the conversation at this point? Anything? Is there a way you can help this person through what you do; maybe put them in touch with another connection of yours if there is some real opportunity? Have you perhaps gleaned something that could be stored in your head for a later date?

Part of networking with others is to make connections for later, or to introduce someone to another connection of yours when the opportunity arises. Store as much information as you can about the person in one of those pigeonholes in your head to use as and when the opportunity arises. We never actually forget anything; we simply can't recall it at the moment we need it, so we think we have forgotten it. But if you ask your unconscious computer to work on it and give you the answer by a certain time frame, you will find in most cases it will. The information you're trying to recall does come to you. I use this trick more and more often as I get older!

I'd like to share with you Lisa's story about being in the right place at the right time, doing a great job and being gently persistent.

Lisa's story

About six weeks ago I entered my company, HRtoolkit, in the local Westpac Bank Business Awards. I handed in the entry on Tuesday to my local chamber of commerce, which was administering the awards. On the Thursday, unbeknown to me, Jo-Anne, a chamber staff member, asked of the office in general, 'I want to restart the employment law update seminars. Does anyone know who would be good at doing this?' Rebecca, who had my entry on her desk, suggested HRtoolkit, and another person in the office who receives my newsletter also suggested us.

On the basis of this double endorsement Jo-Anne called me and asked if I would be interested in presenting at the employment law update seminars for the chamber of commerce. Of course I said yes, and when I met with her she explained that she wanted me to run the seminars for the next couple of years…absolutely fantastic exposure for my business and bottom line!

About four weeks later we ran the first seminar and it went really well.

Off the back of the success of the seminar Jo-Anne spoke to the chamber's CEO about HRtoolkit and the seminars and suggested that this would be exactly the kind of thing they should be offering to all of their members. The CEO agreed and asked to meet with me.

I met with Michael and, at his request, I submitted a proposal for HRtoolkit to take over the chamber's 0800 free phone number.

Lisa's story *(cont'd)*

I think I can safely say it has gone better than planned. We took over the 0800 number; we are looking after all of the employment training seminars (about 12) this year; we have already had several significant new consultancy clients as a direct result of this contract; and, as far as the chamber team is concerned, we are now part of the furniture and integrated as such. This has created even more spin-offs of four other chambers of commerce around the country, which are already dialling into our service, as well as me being interviewed on radio as the 'HR Guru'.

It has certainly helped smooth the way with three significant negotiations, creating even wider opportunities outside the Chamber of Commerce. So overall the direct impact of getting the contract significantly increased my business, and the spin-off in reputation and contacts is huge!

One thing I have since discovered is that, even though I had never previously got an audience with the CEO, my name had registered with him as someone who had been knocking at his door for several years. Serendipity got me there in the end, but years of persistence ensured that my name was not new to him!

So from entering the local business awards, Lisa's business has skyrocketed and her ROI has been many thousands of dollars because she followed up, did a great job running the first seminar and her name was already on the CEO's radar because she had been 'knocking at his door' for several years. By lining those elements up...Bingo!—it all came together.

So as we're talking about things happening by chance because someone made a phone call, I have included this great story about how digging deep into your memory to an encounter you had some time ago can save the day for not only you, but for 15 other people as well.

Total recall

Paul was the managing director of an advertising agency in the UK in the 90s. Unbeknown to him at the time, a disagreement between one of his account directors and a key client that equated to one-third of their business resulted in the client resigning their account overnight. One-third of their business was lost just like that, with no hope of recovery.

They struggled to fill the business gap for two long years, but their revenue had gone from more than two million dollars to just over one million dollars and the bank was breathing down their neck. They still had overheads. What could they do?

They had three choices:

1 Fold the business and walk away.

2 Make everyone redundant and manage the remaining accounts alone.

3 Try to grow the business.

Trying to grow the business seemed to be the most ridiculous option as they had been trying to do that for the past two years without success, so what was going to change now?

Then Paul had a thought. He recalled a meeting he had had with Tony, an account manager at a print company, some years earlier, and made the decision to call him that night and ask him about an idea he had in mind.

Paul knew that Tony had been in charge of a large account when they first met. He asked Tony if he still handled the account and Tony said yes. He also asked him if the

Total recall *(cont'd)*

company he worked for had a working contract for this account and he said no. Then Paul offered him a part of his business and a job if Tony could help to transfer and secure the account to his business. Again Tony said yes. The next day, Paul was on a train heading to London to meet the client and, one month later, the client transferred two million dollars worth of business across to his agency, and this quickly grew to more than three million dollars.

Paul later sold his shareholding in the company and moved on, having learned some tough lessons. He should have known about the account director's disagreement with their key client, which had resulted in the loss of such a big part of his business. Had he not recalled meeting Tony and phoned him that night, the outcome could have been very different. Instead, 15 people were able to keep their jobs and Paul and the other directors rebuilt the agency.

Paul had an idea, acted on it swiftly and picked up the phone to say hello. The ROI on recalling a conversation with a connection from way back was more than three million dollars. Disaster was averted, lessons were learned and it was a great outcome for his team as no-one lost their job.

Act on it

There is a well-known tale about a man struggling to save himself from drowning after heavy rains swelled the local river and it burst its banks. He was clinging on to the roof of his house as the waters rushed by when a man in a rowing boat shouted to him to jump in.

'No, thank you. I am praying to God. He will save me.'

Soon after, a motorboat came by and the driver asked him to jump aboard, to which he replied, 'No, thank you. I am praying to God. He will save me.'

Then a helicopter flew over, a rope was lowered and a man shouted down to him, 'Come aboard.' The stranded man again said, 'No, thank you. I am praying to God. He will save me.' The helicopter flew away.

Not long after, the man slid into the water and drowned.

When he arrived in heaven, he asked God, 'What happened? I prayed to you that you would save me, and yet here I am: dead.'

'Well,' said God. 'I sent you a rowing boat, a motorboat and a helicopter. What more did you want?'

The moral of the story? Take opportunities as they arise.

Charlotte's story is a prime example of acting on a sign and seeing where it takes you—in this case, a career change from hairdressing to human resources.

Charlotte's story

In my family, university was never really seen as an option, and so we were encouraged to get a trade. I had done really well at school (even gaining merits in sixth form) but because of the way my family was I went on to complete a hairdressing apprenticeship and manage a bar. Following this I set off on my overseas experience to London and found a nice live-in position at a pub in Haymarket.

The pub was around the corner from a management consultancy's head office and almost every day after work I'd pull pints and have a friendly chat with the operations manager and other staff from the offices.

Charlotte's story *(cont'd)*

A few months into the job, I decided it was time for me to move on from the pub.

The day before I was finishing up I saw Peter, the operations manager, looking worried and asked him what was wrong. He mentioned that he had just had someone pull out from a project administration role for a large outplacement project about to start with a key client. At that moment he looked up at me and said, 'You're meant to be leaving. Do you want to take on the role?'

I told him I would love to but I didn't have any specific experience. Peter said he felt he knew me from our chats over the previous few months. He said that on gut instinct he knew I was right for the role and he trusted me to do the work.

So, on that leap of faith I worked for that management consultancy in the UK and found my passion for HR and people development. I went back home and knew I wanted to continue to grow my career in this direction. I've now completed studies while working in both the human resources and the learning and development fields and haven't looked back.

So, from pulling pints, by building a relationship with a customer and taking a leap of faith when she saw the sign, Charlotte was able to make a significant career change. It took guts to make the move from her original plan to go and try a job she knew absolutely nothing about, but her pub customer obviously thought he knew her well enough and that her skills were relevant to the position he needed to fill. ROI for Charlotte: a life-changing experience as well as a considerable increase in income.

Heather found herself in a situation that seemed to drop from the sky.

Acting on a brief encounter

After returning from 10 years abroad, Heather went to a function with her parents at the local school where they taught. She bumped into a woman she vaguely knew as she was the sister of someone Heather had gone to school with. The woman informed her that she wanted to leave her job tutoring at the local university, and that Heather would be a perfect replacement for the role. She insisted that Heather apply for the job.

A week later, Heather had a job tutoring accounting to university students, which from that point on has seen tutoring and training as a core component of the services she offers. Since that day, she has never heard from or seen the woman again.

Talk about chance! Heather wasn't even looking for an opportunity when it presented itself. But she acted on it and gained employment as a result.

When a chance comes your way, you may not even be looking for the opportunity it could bring you, so when it does come along act on it and see where it takes you. It could well be life changing.

Chapter 3

Find the commonality

The longer we listen to one another—with real attention—the more commonality we will find in all our lives. That is, if we are careful to exchange with one another life stories and not simply opinions.

Barbara Deming

The theme of having something in common with an unknown person runs through this book because I believe it's the single most important way to get luck, fate, serendipity—or whatever you prefer to call it—working for you. Being in search of serendipity is definitely a contradiction in terms, but why not give it a bit of a shove to see what happens?

Walking up to someone and saying hello may seem a bit strange to the other person unless you have something in common, such as standing in an elevator together. Finding common ground in a situation is an acceptable reason to make a connection without looking like a nutter.

Inside church, for example, where the common interest is to pray, saying a quick 'hi' to another person along the pew is socially acceptable because you both belong to the same church. At a rock concert, it's okay to chat to the person next to you about the band because you're both there to experience the music. At a football match when your team is losing, it's okay to moan and groan to the person in front of you about the team's poor performance today and reminisce about the glory days because you both love the team.

At a conference, we're quite happy to talk to other people in the coffee queue at interval time about how great the last session was because, again, you have something in common. Smokers will stand out in the freezing cold weather to get their 10-minute nicotine fix and chat to other smokers from different departments at the office, because of commonality.

Rare-car drivers will flash their lights at other drivers of a similar rare car by way of a greeting. Harley riders will nod to other Harley riders and scooter riders will do the same.

As a runner, I have often noticed that dog walkers will greet other dog walkers, but not runners; runners will acknowledge other runners but not cyclists; and cyclists will only nod to other cyclists and not dog walkers. Round and round it goes. There is virtually no cross-activity greeting, only same-activity. I have witnessed this many times and it always fascinates me. Commonality is the key reason that talking to a stranger is acceptable.

Perhaps it is human nature that having something in common with another person makes us feel happy to strike up a conversation. Two teenagers who don't know each other wouldn't normally start talking at a checkout queue, unless perhaps they noticed they were wearing the same cult T-shirt under their jackets.

Back out on the street, we walk along with our heads down, eyes averted, headphones plugged in or playing with our smart phones, all the time avoiding contact with anyone else. Whether we're simply trying to get from A to B as quickly as possible, or shopping in the mall, it's pretty much the same scenario—we want to avoid any contact. Perhaps it's because attempting to find out if we have commonality with everyone we pass in the street would be unrealistic.

Imagine if we could find commonality with a few more people around us. How much more enriched our lives would be if one day we met someone who took us on a journey, whether business or pleasure, which we would otherwise have missed out on, had that chance encounter never happened.

John shares a great example of friendship that was born because two people found something in common late one night, both weary after a flight and waiting for their baggage at the airport baggage carousel.

John's story

A few years ago I arrived home late on a Saturday evening to our small local airport. I was waiting for my luggage when a gentleman with a strange accent lamented to me that all of the rental car agencies had closed down for the evening. He asked me where the taxis were, and I informed him that at that hour of the night (11 pm) there most likely weren't any taxis around.

I asked him where he was going and it turned out it was just a few kilometres from my home—and a fairly long ride from the airport. So I told him I'd be happy to give him a ride to his hotel since there was little chance he would find a taxi and his hotel was on the way to where I was going anyway. He was politely reluctant, but realised the predicament he was in and accepted.

I called my wife, who was on her way to pick me up, and informed her we'd be giving a stranded traveller a ride to his hotel. When my wife arrived we put our new friend's luggage in the back of our SUV and jumped in to head for the hotel. As is our custom, my wife had brought some wine and cheese for me to enjoy after the

John's story *(cont'd)*

long flight home, which was much to the surprise of our guest who was somewhat overwhelmed to be offered a nice New Zealand Sauvignon Blanc and appetisers on the ride to his hotel!

Along the way we asked him how he was going to get back to the airport to pick up his rental car the next morning and when he said he would take a taxi, we told him we would pick him up the next morning for breakfast and run him to the airport as it was near where we normally have breakfast on weekends.

The next morning we picked up Cameron—our new Australian best friend—and took him to a traditional southern breakfast where he tried grits for the first time (and was not particularly impressed with them!).

When we dropped him off at the airport to pick up his rental car we invited him to come over for dinner the next evening, and as he had no plans he quickly accepted. It turned out that Cameron was in town to close a business deal for his small Australian company and would likely be coming back on an annual basis to meet with his client, so we told him to please stay in close touch.

About six months later Cameron was back in town and we took him to an American football game at our university, the University of Florida, which happens to be one of the most amazing football experiences in America. More than 100 000 people attend each game and the party before and after the game is beyond comprehension. We had several friends who were throwing big 'tailgate' parties and we enjoyed showing Cameron how Americans celebrate a football weekend.

I also called in a few favours and got tickets right down on the edge of the field where Cameron was able to see just how big and fast American college football players are.

That was about three years ago, and we have kept in close touch ever since. This coming year I have been asked to give a series of speeches across Australia and am so excited that Cameron has invited us to his town, his company and his home to enjoy some fantastic Australian hospitality.

We have so enjoyed our friendship over the past few years, which is now blossoming into the chance to do work together and for him to introduce us to all of his friends.

As someone who travels as many as 200 days a year I know what it's like to get stuck in a strange place late at night so it was a pleasure to help a fellow traveller, a pleasure which through serendipity has now given my wife and me a great new friend and business colleague.

Although John's new travelling friend, Cameron, was reluctant at first to take up the offer of a lift to his hotel, accepting turned out to be a wise move, not only for getting to his destination and a bed for the night, but also for finding new friends and possible future business connections. Sometimes you just click with someone, and as in Cameron and John's case, a friendship and connection develops. I bet after having great seats at that football game in Florida, Cameron has told as many of his friends as possible about the great guy he met at the baggage carousel late one night. ROI for John and Cameron: a new friend and business connection.

Try this

What are all the things that interest you that you would notice in others? Think about your sports, your music, your fashion and all your other interests. When you recall the things you are interested in, you will notice these areas more in others, making it easier to see the commonality.

Commonality is something that instantly ignites a flicker in us because it means we share a common interest in something with someone. Think about that moment when you discover you both know the same person, or you went to the same university. You instantly take more notice and your interest in that person changes. Find the commonality wherever you can.

Chapter 4

How behaviour determines outcomes

In order to be irreplaceable one must always be different.

Coco Chanel

The way people behave in situations where they have the opportunity to make new acquaintances is interesting to observe. Some people are a bit more 'out there' in their approach and will feel quite comfortable striking up a conversation with just about anyone. Others need a little extra help in that department and may not feel confident about saying hello to a stranger.

Be a bit 'out there'

I want to tell you about a guy named Scott Ginsberg, also known as 'the nametag guy' because he wears a nametag all the time. Scott is no shrinking violet, and he's more than happy to chat to other people anytime. His label came about when he started his own social experiment to make friends.

Scott's story

It started as an experiment. I wanted to see what would happen if I wore a nametag out in the street and in other public places. So I wore it 24 hours a day, seven days a week.

One day I met a guy on a bus who asked about my nametag. Turns out, he had a friend who was an editor at a local paper. He told her about me, she looked me up, and then she interviewed me. That interview launched my career.

I now have my name tattooed on my chest so it's permanently there on display, no matter what I'm doing—I've actually been wearing my nametag now for more than 4000 days.

Scott has made a career out of wearing his nametag. He is now a writer, professional speaker and business consultant showing companies how to make a name for themselves. I don't know of anyone else who does exactly what Scott does in the way he does it. It really is his point of difference, or as Seth Godin would say, his Purple Cow.

Imagine wearing a name badge on your jacket for all to see each and every day. Imagine how many people would wonder why you're wearing it to the coffee shop or the shopping mall, and then imagine how many chance conversations you would encounter because of it. It's a great conversation icebreaker, and it would really pique people's curiosity—it certainly would mine.

I asked Scott what advice he would give other people who want to give something like this a go.

'People will ask why, so have an answer ready. Be prepared for some strange looks and jokes and other accompanying frustrations. But it's worth it to meet cool people.'

So it works for Scott, and he's made a business out of doing it. Because he's bold, happy for people to enquire and loves meeting people who do ask questions, he now teaches others how to make a name for themselves.

The ROI for Scott wearing a nametag 24/7 is huge because he has made a business out of doing this. This has probably run into the hundreds of thousands — if not millions — of dollars over the past 11 years, and will surely continue to rise.

What Scott does to engage with others is totally different from what I talked about in the previous chapter about finding a common thread, but it works just as effectively in starting a conversation.

You don't need to be quite so obvious in your endeavours to meet new people, and indeed I think it takes a particularly strong person to do what Scott does, but if it fits in with your personality, why not?

I should imagine he has some very cool stories to tell from the hundreds of thousands of people he has met over the past 11 years he has been wearing a nametag.

So, I've now ordered a nametag for myself, and I will wear it each day that I am out to see what happens — a sort of in-between commitment to wearing it continually or not at all.

Are you the right person to pull off something like that? Do you have the right behavioural profile for it?

Behavioural profiles

Behavioural profiles are all pretty much based on a four-point quadrant. Whether it be letters, shapes, animals or something else, they are all based on the same concept of four areas.

Dr Gary Couture created a version using birds—a dove, an owl, a peacock and an eagle—but I prefer the simplicity and clarity of DiSC® profiling where you are either a D, an I, an S, a C or a combination of these. You could be in just one part of the quadrant or a mixture of several areas, but I think it's important to note that not every profile type would find it easy being as 'out there' as Scott. For example, being a little 'out there' does not suit every behavioural style. Depending on which part of the quadrant their behaviour falls into, some people will feel more comfortable than others about being a little 'out there'. Many people may well feel totally overwhelmed if asked to wear a nametag all the time, and may do their utmost to keep away from such situations.

Someone like Scott, who has a large amount of confidence, would feel comfortable talking about himself when people ask, 'Why?' because he has a great sense of fun. The same cannot be said for someone at the other side of the quadrant, someone who is very private, concerned about offending people and thinks the whole nametag idea is ridiculous. Being that bold is not for everyone.

Figure 4.1 gives you an idea of what the DiSC® quadrant looks like. You may be able to identify which part of the quadrant you sit in right off if you are very strong in one area. If nothing sticks out to you immediately, you could be a mixture of more than one area. Many people are a combination.

DiSC® is based on these four quadrants: dominance, influence, steadiness and conscientiousness. I am a mixture of three areas, a pretty even split between I and S with a little bit of C, which roughly means I want to be friends with everyone, I talk a lot and I can be a bit reserved, with no D for Dominance.

I go into more detail on DiSC® profiling in chapter 13.

Figure 4.1: DiSC® profiling

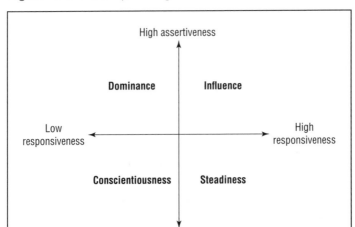

Meanwhile, I'd like to share with you some more stories of people who like to be a bit different. Isabelle, like Scott, is also a bit 'out there'. She loves to wear a fedora and finds it really creates a talking point.

Isabelle's story

For me, it's hats. I love hats, wear them quite often and in a world where a baseball cap is considered appropriate headwear, proper fedoras are always a conversation starter. Hat wearers often quietly nod to each other on the street, a way of saying, 'I get you; we're of the same tribe…and nice feather by the way.' After a recent purchase, I gave the address of the hat shop to at least three strangers on the street and in elevators. It's also a good icebreaker at parties. Inevitably, a non–tribe member will steal your hat and try it on. That's how we make converts, and it always brightens up a boring elevator ride or coffee run.

So that's the simple story about how a woman with a love for fedoras has found a way to get people to notice her and chat about hats, albeit not intentionally. Isabelle's hats certainly have become a talking point.

Andrew is another example of someone a little more 'out there' who achieved great business success via a series of conversations involving a whole string of people.

Trainspotting

Andrew is in the recruitment industry and a few years ago he was asked by a client to recruit a PR manager. This led to him being introduced to Chris, who shared the same 'acquired-taste' sense of humour as Andrew and they just clicked. Chris unfortunately didn't get the job but, some weeks later, he was stuck on a train and ended up sharing a bottle of wine with a fellow traveller called Stuart. They too clicked and Andrew's name popped up in their conversation, so Chris introduced Stuart to him the next day.

Stuart invited Andrew to the soccer in an executive box followed by a noodle supper later on and it was there that Andrew met a fellow guest called Craig. Craig just happened to be struggling to appoint a new marketing manager, and he hired Andrew to get the position filled.

During his search for a candidate for the position, Andrew met Ian, who didn't get the job but really enjoyed meeting Andrew and introduced him to his HR director, Stephanie. The end of the story and the serendipitous moment was that Stephanie became Andrew's biggest ever client! Had the train not been delayed, the wine not been opened, the football game and the following noodle supper not been attended and all the conversations not taken place it may simply never have happened.

After the initial meeting between Chris and Andrew, the common thread that these two people had was being stuck on a train, and one of them making the first move to say hello.

The ROI for Andrew: tens of thousands of dollars.

Be open to subtlety

In contrast to 'out there' approaches are chance encounters that have taken place due to a series of really subtle events—nothing quite as obvious as Scott's approach, but stumble-upon moments all the same.

Serendipity on the phone

Alistair made a telephone call to book a birthday event for one of his children and ended up talking to the business owner about the economy and business in general. The serendipitous moment occurred when the business owner asked him what he did for a living and, on finding out he was a small-business adviser, engaged his services to help her, and so he ended up working with her and her business.

The ROI for Alistair: several hundred dollars.

The same subtle events were in play for Bob one morning at the office.

A reward just for saying hello

Bob got to the office early one morning to get his work underway before the rest of the team arrived. The telephone rang and he answered it to find someone looking for a colleague who had recently left their employment. They got chatting, and it turned out the person calling was referred by his father-in-law and was in the market for nearly one million dollars of financing. Was he able to help? Of course he was, so that's what they did.

From there, the gentleman's father-in-law called to thank him for doing such a great job, and he has continued to give him referrals. The ROI for Bob: more than three million dollars and rising.

All of this stemmed from being in the office early, taking the phone call and saying hello. The benefits for Bob of doing his best to help the person on the other end of the line were immense. Getting in early can have its benefits. Serendipitous moments happen all the time; we may not notice them but they are there. The path ahead each and every day depends on us seeing the signs and acting on them: a chance telephone call, a woman in the elevator with a hat just like yours or sharing a bottle of wine with a stranger while you're stuck on a train are all opportunities to make new acquaintances. And there will be more.

Chapter 5

Sameness creates comfort, difference creates opportunity

In other words, I would be giving in to a myth of sameness which I think can destroy us.

Audre Lorde

I believe life is very much like a kaleidoscope; when you shake things up a little, you see a different picture. So why not try to make some simple changes to your routine to give yourself a chance of stumbling across something or someone fresh and exciting?

A story of my own

I live on a fig orchard, and in the autumn months I lend a hand picking the fruit each morning before the birds get to them, which, when the sun is shining, is lovely; when it's wet, definitely not so!

Each morning, I would walk up and down the rows searching for ripe fruit, and I always did the same rows in the same order: down the right side, and back up the left side. One afternoon after I had picked my rows, I had reason to walk down the rows again, but I walked down

---

> ## A story of my own *(cont'd)*
>
> the left side of the row, the opposite way from earlier on in the day, and noticed that I had missed a quantity of ripe fruit. How could that be? It was only a few hours ago that I had picked all of the ripe fruit, hadn't I? Then it dawned on me that because I was looking at the rows from a different view I had seen all of the fruit that was 'hiding' under leaves and branches, fruit that I couldn't see by walking in the other direction. But it was there, and if I didn't pick it, it would go to waste.

Since my realisation of possibly letting great quantities of fruit spoil, I often think of this analogy when I do other tasks out of routine. What am I missing that is there, hiding from me just because I have a set routine?

Mix it up a bit

Jumbling things up a bit and putting yourself in a different situation is like a game of roulette. Where will the ball land? What will happen because of your actions? Who will you come into contact with? What might you see that you have never seen before? And what might you learn?

There is an accountancy firm in town that has a rule about where their employees can and can't eat their lunch. No-one is allowed to eat at their desk; they must make the effort to either sit in the lunchroom with the other team members, or go out. This is for a very simple reason. You won't meet anyone new sitting at your desk eating!

Everyone wants new clients, right? This firm has made the rule because everyone knows someone who uses an accountant. So why not make use of each and every team member to get the firm's brand name out there and be talked about when possible?

Some simple things you could consider changing are:

- Go to a different coffee shop each day and take note of the people in there. You may recognise someone you once knew or see someone you would like to know.

- Park on a different street occasionally.

- Get your petrol from a different filling station.

- Stand in a different place on the sideline this weekend.

- Try a different takeaway restaurant next time.

All of these are very simple things to put into place to heighten your chances of seeing something or someone new.

Look out for opportunities to mix things up a little, such as taking a night-school class, as Cheryl did.

Subtle serendipity

Cheryl began something new by taking writing classes and soon discovered that one of her classmates lived in her neighbourhood, so they started to share the same taxi home after classes.

One evening while on the way home in the taxi, Cheryl mentioned that she was selling her house. It had been on the market for some time, and she was selling it because it was simply too big for her now as it was on 12 acres and had a pool to keep up. That was the end of the conversation until the following week when she received an email from her friend asking if there were any photos available online so that she and her family could take a look. Cheryl sent them the agent's website link to her property. Smitten, they asked if they could view the

Subtle serendipity *(cont'd)*

property that weekend. 'Sure, bring your swimsuits. The weekend weather promises to be lovely.' They did, they swam and they fell in love with the house.

They did look at other houses, but went back to Cheryl's place for another look before making her an offer, which she accepted. The house was sold subject to inspection from a chance conversation sharing a taxi ride home!

The ROI for Cheryl was that her house sold, enabling her to move on quickly. And all because she decided to try something new.

Putting yourself in different situations and dropping seemingly irrelevant things into the conversation can have a profound effect on the outcome if the serendipity gods are all lined up and ready to make things work out. If you don't first give them the ammunition to work with, it's never going to happen.

Neat or nutty?

You're sure to come across some 'out there' ideas for creating stumble-upon moments and, even though they may sound nutty on the surface, consider them for whether they could actually be great ideas and not nutty at all.

For example, an idea came to me after seeing a Facebook post by someone who had decided that a plane flight had the possibility of being a whole lot more productive than just sitting quietly on his own, working, reading or watching a movie.

Many businesspeople take long journeys as part of their work. Whether that journey is on a plane, a train or perhaps a bus, there are likely to be other businesspeople on board filling their time in the same manner.

Why not, then, at the time of boarding and walking to your seat, hold up a sign that says 'business help here' or 'insurance advice here' or 'spiritualist available now' so that you can choose who you sit next to and strike up a conversation — one that may just lead to some good for both of you?

It only sounds nutty because no-one is doing it, but I bet you would have some takers.

Try this

If you feel brave enough to make the first move and hold up a sign, go for it. I would be interested in the response you get so do let me know.

Dutch airline KLM has had a similar idea with an initiative called 'Meet and Seat'. It enables people to choose who they sit next to on the plane using Facebook. It's more than a seat selector in that you can see a photo of possible 'row mates' to spend your journey with. If you find the thought of sitting next to someone who has 'chosen' you for the entire journey not to your liking, you don't have to take part. The program is 'opt in', so you would have to download the 'Meet and Seat' app, but it does have its advantages. For example, if you've been at a conference or trade show for two days, it may be beneficial to share the journey home and chat to other attendees about the event rather than being stuck next to someone who talks about their poodle the whole way.

Taking this idea a bit further, you may frequent a coffee shop that has large communal tables as well as the regular smaller ones. I personally like to use these tables if they're available because you never know who you'll be sitting with and you may just start with hello and get chatting about something useful. Lots of people who work from home offices like to step out and work from a coffee shop occasionally, so communal tables are your chance to 'put your sign up' and see what happens. As long as you're buying coffee, I'm sure the café owner won't mind, but you may want to check. Coffee shops are great places to strike up a brief conversation; after all, you're all waiting in line for the same thing, right? You have a common thread.

Why not try putting your sign up to see what response you get? With the coffee shop owner's permission, you may be able to run a regular 'clinic', say once per month, which could be a great way of meeting new prospects.

Graeme's coffee shop experience was a little different.

Coffee shock

Graeme was in a coffee shop when he overheard a group of people dressed in their work uniforms talking about a disciplinary matter and how they were going to handle it, among other staff issues. When he got back to his office he contacted the HR manager at their head office and suggested to them that those sorts of conversations were not meant to be held in a coffee shop environment where he and others were able to overhear every word.

From there, the conversation developed and resulted in Graeme actually doing some consultancy work for this well-known brand and to this day he is still known to them as 'the guy from the café'.

The ROI for Graeme was several thousand dollars, and a change in procedure for the company involved.

Something good came out of something negative, but the main point is that because Graeme picked up the phone and spoke to head office the conversation took place and something positive ensued.

All it takes is an icebreaker

I said hello to a chap this morning as we both flicked through a copy of the daily paper waiting for our takeaway coffee, and ended up having a giggle. We may never see each other again, but we could just as easily bump into each other in the future and our 'ice' is already broken. You only need an opener along the lines of 'Boy, am I ready for my coffee this morning' and generally you will find you get a warm response from the person waiting in line with you. Just start with hello.

What about using the same idea at some of the networking events you attend, particularly if you're an organiser? Why not suggest an icebreaker session, something along the lines of speed networking? This is when all the attendees very quickly get to meet and say hello to everyone else in the room over a short period of time. For example, if the event is to take up two hours, you may ask everyone to speed network for 10 minutes. The remaining time is then used more productively than if the attendees had not yet had a chance to meet because the attendees are likely to spend it circling back to those people they are keen to talk to some more.

Most networking events leave it up to the attendees to connect with someone and say hello. This can make it difficult to meet everyone in the room and you may not actually get to say hello to the person in the room you would really want to meet because you don't know they are even there. Unless you flit around the room like a mad thing, quickly looking at everyone's nametag, that's about your only option for finding out more about them.

I go to the hairdresser regularly to get my hair cut and coloured. It's always a slow and boring process, taking about two hours on average for even my short hair. We all sit staring at ourselves in the mirror with our backs to each other, lined up along two walls, in silence. I am of the age where it's getting too hard to read without glasses so I can't even read to pass the time and I'm usually bored to tears by the end of it.

It's likely the other ladies in the salon feel the same way. But does anyone say hello to someone else? Does anyone strike up a conversation? No. Although I think the experience could be made a whole lot more pleasurable, interesting and even more productive if someone did. Maybe if the salon owner picked up on this and made an effort to get a discussion flowing among the clients — making the idea of going to the hairdresser a fun one where you can make new friends along the way and have a giggle at the same time — it wouldn't be such a chore but a social event to look forward to. What a great talking point or point of difference from the salon's brand perspective too. It doesn't have to be boring and quiet. In fact, here's a story about a serendipitous moment in a salon.

Connecting with cats

During a cut and blow-wave appointment at her local salon, Anne was talking to her hairdresser about her cat, which she wanted to impregnate. Another client, Tia, overheard her and said she had a very good-looking tomcat and would Anne be interested in 'borrowing' him for a while? A litter of kittens and 45 years later, they are still the best of friends!

That was quite a serendipitous moment—and what a way to make a friend (which, it could be argued, is worth more than any amount of money) as well as realising a wish of having a litter of kittens.

Try this

How many times do you pass the same person waiting patiently for their bus each morning as you drive by? You're both going in the same direction, so why not ask them if they would like a lift?

When I was commuting from Winchester in the south of England into London Victoria every day, I, like many other commuters on the train platform, stood pretty much in the same spot each day and entered the same carriage each day. Looking back now, it seems so sad and mundane, but thousands of people do it daily.

The other passengers in my particular carriage decided that, as they saw the same commuters daily, why not make the journey more fun and interesting? So, people began to get out of their seats and walk around, chatting to others, some holding a takeaway coffee, swapping stories. Gradually, over time, it became a social part of the day rather than the drudge and boredom that it had been. At Christmas, the wine would flow on the return journeys in the evening and everyone had a distinct festive spirit. It became almost like a social club, complete with arranged outings and other events. The passengers in that carriage could well have carried on their daily journey to the city like every other person on the train, and I often wonder what serendipitous events were created with the many conversations that went on back then.

I have never experienced anything quite like that on any other regular transport service, and I hope it's still continuing on that Winchester-to-Victoria line all these years later.

So remember, while carrying on in the same manner does give you a feeling of comfort it's getting out of your comfort zone and approaching something in a different way that will provide you with opportunities to meet new people and discover new things.

Part summary

From early on in our lives we're taught to keep away from people we're not familiar with, which really goes against the grain of what we need to do as we start out in our working lives: communicating with others. We need to move away from the apron strings, but as young adolescents it can be nerve-racking; we just don't have enough confidence at that age. No-one taught us at school that who we know is just as important as what we know and that life will be just one long series of connections and relationships. No-one mentioned that interacting with others could prove to be so valuable in our future success. Now we have to make strides ourselves to make that happen, and we can only do this by making a conscious effort to get things moving in the right direction.

The easiest way to have a conversation with anyone is to start with hello—it's just good manners. From there we can find the commonality to branch the conversation out in a particular direction that's both enjoyable and non-threatening.

You can come across commonality in many ways: the person using the same Montblanc pen as you, the coffee shop (we all need a coffee at some time), the train platform (getting on the same train) or the lunch queue at a conference (when we've all been listening to the same speakers). Wherever it is, the commonality is the thing to focus on—finding that one thing that you both share always works.

For anything to happen, you must first take action. It's no good just thinking about it—you must put yourself in a common situation. You won't get very far sitting behind your desk all day. Think about all the people you come across each day right now: the people at the bus stop, in the elevator, the lobby, the coffee shop, the lunch shop...the list goes on, and there are people in each and every one of these places you frequent every day who you know absolutely nothing about. And just possibly, someone, somewhere could hold the key to getting your next idea off the ground, be it in relation to your next employer or even your future partner.

Think also about mixing up your daily routine by getting your lunch from a different store, eating it in the park instead of at your desk and parking around the corner from the office and walking that little bit. By mixing your routine you open yourself up to a whole new set of people to say hello to.

Look for the subtle chances that appear, such as telephone calls that you answer on behalf of someone else, or an invitation to sit at your rotary president's table at lunch, or a smile or greeting from a fellow commuter. Not all opportunities will be obvious, but they all need your attention and action in order to make things happen.

Don't boo hoo the ideas that on the surface may seem a little nutty. Just because no-one else is doing it doesn't mean it's not a good idea. So if you want to put a sign up while you wait for your flight in the business lounge at the airport and give someone a little free advice, go for it!

In a nutshell

- 'Never talk to strangers' is not necessarily the right advice in the adult world. A stranger is simply someone you haven't met yet.

- Are we giving ourselves enough opportunities to experience moments of serendipity? Probably not, so be aware of the knowledge, music and people we came across in places we used to frequent that are sadly in decline, such as bookstores, and make up for them with an alternative.

- Action really does bring activity, so plan in time or places when or where you could meet new people easily.

- Commonality is by far the simplest icebreaker conversation starter and an easy way is to start with hello, so look to find the obvious stand-out commonality between you and a person you'd like to get to know.

- If being a little more 'out there' fits your personality, then try doing something like Scott 'the nametag guy' or Isabelle with her fedoras.

- Mix your routine up to see what else the kaleidoscope of life has to offer you. Who might you meet by changing your coffee shop or grocery store?

- Nutty ideas can be fun so if you're feeling brave, give it a go. Stick your sign up and see what happens.

Part II

How to start a productive conversation with a stranger

For most people, after that initial hello it can be difficult to know what to talk about with someone new. You don't want to talk about yourself—that would be rude and boring—and you don't want to go into sales pitch mode and chat about your widget, but you do need to say something. In this part of the book we're going to discover positive ways of behaving and continuing a conversation after that first hello.

Read the following chapters to learn how to:

- create the right first impression and understand other people's eye contact
- network freestyle
- decide who you want to talk to and how to start
- start an easy conversation with a complete stranger
- make sure you're networking in the right places for the people you want to meet.

Chapter 6

Making a positive first impression

I don't like that man. I must get to know him better.

Abraham Lincoln

Imagine this scene: you're walking along the beach with your dog, taking in the scenery, and you spot a man walking his trusty labrador, which is off the lead. The man throws a stick to his dog and off the dog bounds, straight into the water to retrieve it, bringing it back to his master with pride. You also notice a woman walking in the opposite direction with her labrador, also off the lead and having a good time with a ball. As the two people and their two dogs get closer, a couple of things could happen. The dogs could run at each other and attack or, if they are well mannered and well trained, they would probably sniff each other out doggy style. You stand for a while, watching out of fascination. What will happen?

The two dogs spot each other and run forwards to investigate each other a bit further. As they approach, a little bit of caution is visible, but only for a second—then it's a full-on sniff-a-thon! Sniffing each other's noses, bodies and rear ends, they accept each other as okay. When the sniff-a-thon is over, they are great mates, mock fighting, rolling around and generally showing off, having a good time. A friend made. Simple!

Drop those inhibitions

Dogs have no inhibitions. Their owners allow them to socialise with each other and they can usually be trusted to play nicely after their initial contact. What great role models well-mannered dogs are to humans for being able to make new friends easily.

Imagine if we acted the same way. What would people think? I'm not talking about sniffing each other out—that would be weird—but simply getting along so well so quickly without inhibition. We've been brought up to act in a certain way, following unwritten rules that tell us we mustn't fool around like children but show a friendly and reserved exterior. Yet dogs and kids socialise and play with each other easily and have no inhibitions. It's only when adults are introduced to each other that the dynamics change and so we conform to fit in.

Open your eyes and smile

I was once the store general manager for an optical chain in the UK, where I worked with one of the best teams I've encountered in my career. One of the lab technicians was a young man called Danny who, as well as being quite a shy individual, was very kind. If I ever went into his laboratory to check on stock levels of a particular lens for a customer, he would help me find it, laughing jokily because he could always find it well before I could. Every time he did this, he'd smile warmly and say, 'Open your eyes, GM.'

I've never forgotten Danny, and I repeat his saying to myself when I just can't find what I'm looking for. Sometimes we have to look a bit higher or lower than we're accustomed to looking.

I thought about Danny's words one morning when I was out running. It seems that whatever we're doing — running, getting the groceries, meeting a client — our eyes are always at a certain level, just high enough to see where we're going and not trip over anything, and just low enough to 'keep ourselves to ourselves'. By walking around with our eyes at this level, we're aware enough of our surroundings that we don't think about looking anywhere else. But if we were to stop what we're doing and look up, lift our eyes just a little higher, we would be able to take in so much more. We'd see how much brighter things are up there, and how much more aware we can be of our surroundings. It's quite a different view, even if we're only raising our eyes by millimetres.

So make a conscious effort every day to raise your head and eyes just a little higher to take in your new surroundings, look at the people around you and see who else is looking at your level.

This is a great exercise to do when you're out and about, at a networking event or just getting your daily coffee (from a different shop occasionally, remember). Make eye contact with others. Unless you're a totally miserable human being, when someone looks directly at you, your natural reaction is to smile as a way of saying, 'I see you'. It's the equivalent of your eyes starting with hello. Contact made.

Try this

Lift your head, and ultimately your eyes, just a little higher as you go about your daily routine and observe how much more you see as well as who you see. The view can be quite different from what you're used to.

Why is eye contact so important?

Numerous studies have shown that people who make higher levels of eye contact with others are perceived as being:

- more dominant and powerful
- more warm and personable
- more attractive and likeable
- more qualified, skilled, competent and valuable
- more trustworthy, honest and sincere
- more confident and emotionally stable.

It's not surprising then that we should try to make more eye contact with people we meet, and not just in business. Remember how powerful it was the first time you looked deeply into your partner's eyes and they into yours—the connection, and how it felt? Well, while you're not looking for the same effect in a business setting, that feeling of connection is what you're after—something that says, 'I like this person'.

Being able to look people in the eye with confidence can help you deliver a great speech, close a sale, woo the ladies, make your authority heard, show empathy to a friend in need and intimidate your enemy—and all with confidence. Soldiers will take off their sunglasses when directly communicating in a conflict situation, animals will stare each other down before one pounces, babies will follow your eyes as you move them, love stories will start as eyes lock across a crowded room and fighters will stare each other down in the ring before the start bell rings. It's just instinct.

The eyes have it

Have you ever wondered what it is about the eyes that make them so important in communication?

The whites of our eyes make it easy to see the iris and pupil, or focal point of the eye, to see where that focal point is looking. Imagine talking to someone who does not have an iris or a pupil, only the white area. You wouldn't know where they were looking, and if someone isn't looking at you during a conversation, how do you know if they are listening?

We've all experienced having a conversation with someone who really makes it obvious that they're not listening to us: the person who checks their mobile phone while you're talking; the person who continually looks over to the door while you're talking; the person who continually tries to butt in with their comments while you're talking. They're all annoying signs that someone is simply not listening.

You can also discover a lot about a person when you look at their eyes. The old saying 'the eyes are the window to your soul' rings true and describes what we can see in a person, for example:

- *eyes glazed over:* boredom

- *evil eye:* anger

- *bedroom eyes:* love or lust

- *shifty eyes:* untrustworthiness

- *bright eyes:* eagerness

- *twinkling eyes:* mischievous

- *dead behind the eyes:* nothing

- *kind eyes:* open and giving.

The eyes don't lie. Even if you train your body language to do so, it's virtually impossible to stop your eyes from telling the truth. It's why poker players will often wear sunglasses during a game to hide their surprise at the hand they have been dealt. It's called a 'tell'.

Try this

Make a point of noticing other people's eyes just a little more and think about what you see in them. What can you read from them?

So if the eyes are the window to our soul or a dead giveaway of what we're really thinking, is that why some people find it so difficult to make real eye contact? Do they feel vulnerable that the person seeking eye contact will see too much? It's quite possible. But as we've seen, it's an important part of communication and we need to be comfortable with it.

So why are some people no good at eye contact? There are a couple of reasons:

- *Insecurity.* Some people lack confidence or feel insecure because of their physical appearance or because they're talking to someone of a higher status than themselves.

- *Something to hide.* If someone is lying to cover something up, keeping their gaze averted in order to keep the truth from showing in their eyes is common. No doubt you've heard someone say, 'Look me in the eye and tell me...' as it takes a practised liar to be able to do so successfully.

Incidentally, eye contact is just that: eye, not eyes. It's virtually impossible to look into both eyes at the same time, so we tend to choose one and look there. You can of course flit from one eye to the other, but if you do this too often, it can become a little annoying for the person you're talking to.

Don't stare

Don't, however, confuse good eye contact with creepy staring. If you linger when looking into someone's eyes for a moment too long, they will begin to feel uncomfortable, and their body language will give this away. The may try to break your eye contact, or make an excuse to leave. Staring is not nice and people don't appreciate it so be careful not to overstep the time limit. If you're trying to make eye contact with someone in a room and they notice you for a second time but don't respond, then drop it. Don't stare again.

Know how much distance to keep

If you're sitting talking to someone you don't know too well, give yourself a little extra space by leaning back slightly and avert your eyes every sentence or so just for a split second so you don't come across as too intense. On the flip side, if you're having a conversation with someone you know well, you may want to lean in a little, particularly if it's of a private nature or to share some warmth with your friend.

Breaking eye contact

When it's time to break eye contact, perhaps to think over your answer before you give it or to dig into the back of your head to find it, always do so to the left or right, never down to the floor. By looking down at the floor you may be giving off a signal of submissiveness, or even a feeling of a lower status — not necessarily what you want to convey, particularly in an interview or during a business pitch.

It's not really hard to make great eye contact with others, so practise with family members and colleagues at work until you feel more comfortable. You want to make the perfect eye contact with a stranger and get the right acknowledgement, not be seen as creepy.

~

Making a great first impression and using the right amount of eye contact will only stand you in good stead to be remembered for all the right reasons. You're making a concerted effort to meet new people and talk to more strangers, and first impressions are key to your success.

Chapter 7

Networking freestyle — make the first move

It's all about people. It's about networking and being nice to people and not burning any bridges.

Mike Davidson

I think most of us realise that by and large humans are naturally friendly towards each other. So keep this first and foremost in your mind when it comes to meeting someone new. It will make your transition into a professional networker much easier.

We'll look at networking events in the next chapter, but as networking freestyle is possibly the easiest way of starting a conversation with a stranger — because we're more likely to have something obvious in common away from the business environment, such as wearing the same hat or sports shirt, or being in the same car club — we'll cover this first.

Networking freestyle is the term I've given to networking off the cuff with those you find around you at a given moment; that is, not at a formal networking event, which you're no doubt accustomed to.

People like people who are similar to them and so are more likely to respond to their efforts because of the commonality they have. This is where freestyle networking comes in.

Decide who you want to talk to

Having the commitment to build your connection base and say hello to more strangers means you'll have to decide who to talk to, including those you happen to bump into because they are next in line in the coffee queue. What about those people with whom, on the surface, you have nothing in common—people you'll meet in communal places such as airport lounges, train stations or the wine store? You actually do have something in common with them; in fact, there are very few situations where we don't share commonality.

Say you've spotted someone you feel you have a connection with—maybe their appearance caught your eye, or their face looked familiar, or they looked at you first. Whatever it was, you've found your target, for want of a better word. It's what you do next that determines how successful you are at reaching out and connecting.

If you can't find anything obvious to use when it comes to making contact with someone, you'll have to start paying attention to the subtler things, which can be equally useful for starting a conversation.

Putting yourself out there and actively meeting new people takes a certain amount of guts. You need to be confident in your approach, and I bet some of you reading this will be thinking, 'It sounds too hard, actually!'

In this section, I want to go through eight principles of making contact with a stranger and address some of the worries you may have.

The eight principles are:

1   *Have a plan in your head.* Decide who you want to talk to. What do you want the outcome to be? What, if anything, do you have in common that is obvious? You may only have one chance at this person, so make it count and be organised in your approach.

2   *Make the first move.* Get into position. If you don't show
    up physically, nothing will happen. Then you need to
    start with hello. Walk on over to the person you wish to
    speak with, but do it subtly.

3   *Pass a comment.* What subtle or obvious thing can
    you use to connect with someone? Do you both have
    the same overnight bag, use the same smart phone or
    are you both reading the same book? You don't want
    to scare them off before you have said anything. Try
    saying, 'I couldn't help but notice . . .' when you start
    the conversation.

4   *Say hello.* Are you able to say hello and introduce
    yourself? If you receive a negative vibe after you've
    passed your initial comment, then maybe wait. It's good
    manners to say hello, so start there.

5   *Discover their occupation.* After you've introduced yourself,
    allow them to respond with their name and occupation.
    Carry on chatting if they are responsive to you. Say
    something along the lines of, 'Tell me more about what
    you do. Have you been doing this for a long time?'

6   *Steer the conversation.* Have an idea where you want the
    conversation to go and try to steer it there. If they're
    reading a business book you could comment on it. Or
    you can ask what line of business they're in; it's an easy
    way to talk shop. You could say, 'I see you're reading a
    Jim Collins book. Have you read *Great by Choice* yet?'

7   *Obtain their contact information.* Ask for a business card
    for the purpose of following up later. Ask, 'May I have
    one of your business cards? I'd like to follow up a little
    later if I may.'

8   *Agree to follow up.* State that you will follow up with
    them at a later date so that they will be expecting
    you to call. Follow up quickly as the more senior

the connection, the quicker they will forget you. Say, 'Thanks for chatting with me, I'll drop you a line with my details by way of a follow-up later on.'

So that's the very simple process. Now let's look at some of the questions you may have about it. These are the most commonly asked questions and concerns.

Common questions about freestyling

Question 1

They're going to think I'm a stalker if I march up to them and start talking to them, aren't they?

Answer

You're quite right. Think about how you would feel if someone marched up to you, tapped you on the shoulder and started talking to you. After you got over the initial shock, your next thought would probably be, 'Who is this person, why are they here and what do they want?' You would instantly be on the defence, and they would instantly be on the back foot with you, so all in all, it's not a very bright or productive way to approach a complete stranger.

Solution

If you see someone you particularly want to chat with because you feel your company or product could help them in some way, you need to take it slowly and follow a process. For example, you may be in the departure lounge at the airport when you first spot them, so the first thing to do is to mentally make your plan. Take note of things such as their dress sense, shoes and suit; what they are reading; or whether they are using a particular gadget such as the new iPhone.

When the plane is ready to board, you could position yourself near them so that you board at a similar time. Try to make eye contact. A simple nod of the head or a brief smile is all you need to do at this point. If they don't return your gesture, they may have missed it, so don't worry too much. Smiling and nodding again would look dumb and be misconstrued if they did in fact see you the first time.

If they do return your initial gesture this is your first chance to make a good impression and at the same time make a point about mentioning something that you noticed from earlier on. This may just be a comment such as 'I notice you write with a Montblanc pen', or 'How nice to see someone using a classic piece to write with. Do you have other pieces from the range too?' They will be impressed that you noticed the beautiful pen sticking out of their top pocket and be even more impressed that you called something they own a 'classic piece', which always goes down well. You also followed your compliment with another question to keep a brief conversation going.

As you are boarding the plane, there may be very little time to chat further at this point, but you've made yourself known in case the chance arises later. If you're lucky enough to find you're seated together on the plane, you can take your conversation to the next level, but if not, you may be able to make contact again at the baggage reclaim or in the taxi queue at your destination. At all times, be respectful in your approach and act on any signs that your new contact doesn't want to chat at this time.

Question 2

I've made the initial contact, and they are responsive to chatting, but how do I move in to tell them about what I do?

Answer

Don't go and blow it by rushing in with your sales pitch. It won't get you very far or be appreciated.

(continued)

Common questions about freestyling *(cont'd)*

Solution

If you have the chance to chat more and you find your-self in, say, a coffee shop or lounge, then after your initial conversation, hold out your hand and introduce yourself. They will no doubt respond, at which time you can enquire what their business is, and what they do for a living. This is another opportunity to learn more about your new connection by asking pertinent questions about their job role or company, so listen to everything they say and respond with intelligent comments or questions where you can. As they talk about their role within the company, think about how you can help them yourself or help someone you know by passing their details on to someone who could do with their help. Invariably, the conversation will come back round to asking what it is you do, which is your chance to give them the highlights. They may then ask you some questions about your role or company also. This is not your chance to steamroll them into submission with your canned sales pitch.

Question 3

How can I start a conversation with someone who is engrossed in their book or report or sitting next to me on a train with their eyes closed?

Answer

You can't.

Solution

There may well be a time a little later on when your neighbour puts their book down for a breather, so wait until the time is right and then you can pass a comment along the lines of, 'I love it when I find a book that's totally riveting. What's yours about?' If the person is asleep, you can say something similar when they wake up such as, 'It's good to take a nap when you can. You must work hard. What is it that you do?'

Of course you'll find yourself in situations where there really is no way to strike up a conversation, or where their body language tells you they just want to be left alone, so respect their space and leave them undisturbed.

Question 4

We only met very briefly, but I would like to follow up and meet them again. How can I do this respectfully?

Answer

Easily, if done well. If you find that once you've made your initial contact, there's simply very little time to take your conversation any further than 'nice pen', you can be honest and say that you recognise them and that they must be very busy, but ask if you can swap business cards as you have an idea that may benefit them or their company. If you don't at this stage know who they are, you can still ask for their business card and say that you'd like to look into a company that has executives with classy Montblanc pens.

(continued)

Common questions about freestyling *(cont'd)*

Remember back to when you originally spotted them in the departure lounge? This was also the time to put your mental plan together about what to say, in what direction you want the conversation to go and what you want to get out of it. Just as a courtroom lawyer has an exact idea what they want to get from a witness and what direction they want the conversation to go in, it needs planning.

Solution

When you have their business card, there are a couple of ways to follow up but, either way, it should be done within two days of your initial connection. The higher up the company the person is, the busier they are, the sooner they are likely to forget you, so don't delay. There are a couple of ways you could follow up:

- *By email.* The big thing to remember here is to be yourself. You just want to put yourself back on their radar, jog their memory that you chatted briefly, and not launch into sales mode or corporate jargon. If you met by the boarding gate and commented on their pen, you could start your email along the lines of:

  'Hi Steve. I found this link to the new Montblanc pieces for this year, and thought you may want to put something on your Christmas list. I hope your business went well the day we met at the airport. I certainly had a very productive day.

  After our brief meeting, I got thinking about how I can help you in any way, and I have a couple of ideas that I'd like to discuss with you if I may. I'll buy the coffee if you're free next week. What day suits you best?'

Keep it relaxed. It's just a way of connecting again and asking for a meeting to chat more.

- *Via LinkedIn.* You can also consider sending a connection request or message through LinkedIn with a similar flavour. The good thing about sending a note through LinkedIn is that it's extremely easy for the receiver to simply click on your name and read all about you and your experience (but you'd better make sure your profile is the best it can be if you choose this route).

- *By telephone.* You have their card with, probably, their direct telephone number so you can give them a call. What you say over the phone will depend on how well you got on at your initial connection, and what was said. I would suggest that, unless it was a really good conversation about how you can help each other, you should send an email. It's much less intrusive and gives your connection an 'out' if they're really not interested. A telephone conversation to a lukewarm connection may do more damage than good at this point, so try 'courting' them more first.

Question 5

I'm so excited that I met them, I just want to jump straight in with how I can help their company. What next?

Answer

Have you heard the saying, 'Slowly, slowly, catch the monkey'? Be cautious and avoid making any mistakes. Think of it as losing weight. Crash diets only work for a very small amount of time and when you go back to normal eating, your weight very often goes back to where it was before. The best and most effective way to lose weight is to do it gradually over time, letting your body adjust along the way.

(continued)

Common questions about freestyling *(cont'd)*

Solution

If you've sent your follow-up message and it has gone unanswered, you could try again because they may not have had time to respond to your original one yet or their spam filters may have grabbed it. If after you have sent another message you still receive no response, be mindful that they may simply not be interested. My tip to you here is if you are following up using a LinkedIn message, try to send it on a Friday as many people surf through LinkedIn at the weekend when they're catching up on less important work matters.

You could also see if they are on Twitter and follow them there with the hope of chipping into a conversation when an opportunity arises.

Question 6

It looks like they're not interested. Is that the end?

Answer

It could be.

Solution

They may not be interested, so bow out graciously. If they agreed to connect on LinkedIn, at least they are a part of your business network Rolodex, and so your virtual or physical paths may cross again one day. If you keep in touch with your connection occasionally, you may have more luck next time they get a note from you. Maybe the time is just not right at the moment.

Part of having a plan of what you want from your new connection is also knowing when to give it up without becoming a nuisance.

Internal networking

If you work for a company and have been eyeing up an internal vacancy that you think would be a good fit for you, you can use the same principles that we have already talked about, but for internal networking situations. You may be thinking, 'What internal networking situations are there?' There probably are quite a few if you think about where your colleagues and co-workers hang out at communal tables at lunchtime, company social events, collaborative groups, the water cooler and the direct working environment that applies to you. Add into the mix festive events such as your annual Christmas party or summer BBQ and you may find there are plenty of opportunities.

If you find yourself invited to an event such as these, the temptation is to go along with your daily work buddies and hang out together with a beer or two because after all it's a social event, but if you're smart and you have a basic strategy, you could find it the best place to be, career-wise.

For example, if your strategy is to work within a different department that you know will soon be hiring, you need to make yourself known to the person doing the hiring and leave a good impression. When you spot this person at the event, you need to take subtle action, so position yourself ready to say hello and start a conversation. You may want to go with the subtle approach and simply pass a comment about something you've noticed about them, such as their watch or their smart phone, and then if they are responsive, go ahead and introduce yourself. As you work for the same company, I think it's fair to say you can be a little more direct than normal, so introduce yourself and follow that up immediately with which department you work for so they know something about you. Remember, it's a social event, so steer clear of shop talk and pick on something else, such as asking what they're doing over the holidays or the coming weekend, but keep it social and relevant. Towards the end of your conversation, bid them farewell and move back to your buddies with the intention of following up again later via email or telephone.

When you follow up, as long as you have made a good impression, it will be easy to reconnect and arrange a time to chat about your future career in their department. From there, it's up to you to do a great job and get that position, but you will have stood yourself in good stead by building a relationship with the appropriate person beforehand.

> ## Try this
>
> So now you understand the concept of looking for key things to start a conversation with, make a mental note of what they might be with the next five people you come into contact with. This practise will tune your antennae for what to look for when you make your first move.

Your family has networks too

Don't discount your extended family for helping you out in some way with your business or career. Once again, the same principles apply, but it will depend on how well you know the person as to whether or not you need to 'create' a conversation starter. You probably won't in many cases.

You may think that your great aunt Mabel or cousin John really wouldn't be much use to your software business, but just remember that they have a circle of friends and acquaintances too that could be made use of. Ask yourself, does your great aunt Mabel or cousin John even know what it is that you do for a living? Or do they know that you're indeed working on getting an angel investor so that you can expand? Don't be afraid to make sure your family knows exactly what it is that you do and don't just assume they wouldn't understand you work in 'computers'. If you apply some of the principles we've talked about here and know when you've said enough, passed out your business card or agreed to follow up, you've covered your extended family nicely.

If you do really struggle starting a conversation with a complete stranger, practise on those you regularly come into contact with and who know you but are not a part of your current or future business circle. Start by simply making eye contact and a quick smile with your butcher, bus driver or barista, then move on to a brief comment such as, 'I can't wait for the weekend. How about you?' The point is you're starting with hello.

If all else fails when it comes to starting a conversation, there's always the weather—something that's common to us all. So go ahead and make the first move!

Chapter 8

Networking at events

The richest people in the world look for and build networks;
everyone else looks for work.

Robert Kiyosaki

Networking well is an art form to be perfected if you want to reap the rewards, which means spending some time learning the tips and tricks to get good at it and not alienate anyone in the process. But how do you know if it works? Ask any successful businessperson if networking works and listen to their stories about the events that have stemmed from starting with hello.

A great place to meet other people is the good old-fashioned networking event that every town has in some way, shape or form for a variety of reasons. Your local chamber of commerce or business association will put on some of these events, and some networking events are privately run groups that may connect over a specific subject such as HR or they may be organised by someone with a keen interest in connecting with others over a glass of wine.

Generally, you don't need to be a member to join, and in fact organisations such as your local chamber of commerce would encourage non-members to come along in the hope that they decide to join them for future events and training, which they also provide. To find the events that are happening in your part of town, simply Google 'networking events' and the town in which you wish to attend and see what pops up. Also, check sites such as www.eventbright.com, which is a great source of networking events as well as training and seminars among other things.

Trust in the bank

Diana was at her local chamber of commerce networking event when the guest speaker did not appear. As a substitute for the speaker, the chairperson set up a spontaneous networking exercise that had everyone moving around meeting the other guests and asking specific questions to get to know them. It was during this exercise that Diana met the manager of a local bank, a bank that was new to her town, who was looking for ways of connecting with the local community.

At that time, Diana was a school fundraiser in the process of setting up an endowment foundation and, at the same time, the bank was actively seeking sponsorship opportunities. How often does a fundraiser meet someone wanting to give away money? The bank then became the founding member of the foundation, enabling them to attract other donors and be hugely successful.

Some time later, Diana left the school to fulfil her dream of running her own PR consultancy, More Than Words, but even before she had established her business, her first client was waiting in the wings. The original bank manager she had met at the event was a trustee for a not-for-profit organisation and thought she would be the right person to help them develop and implement a communications strategy—a dream client for Diana. Five years on, they still enjoy a happy working relationship with each other and Diana's ROI from attending that original networking event has been substantial.

Had Diana not made the effort to attend the event, the two people may never have met. It's well worth going to such events, if only for a short time. You just never know who will be there and who will need what you have to offer at some stage.

I see there are three different types of people when it comes to networking events: those who hate going, those who love going and those who see it as a necessary evil and make themselves go. Personally, I don't mind going at all as I realise it's an easy way to meet new people over either breakfast if it's an early start, or over a glass of wine if it's an after-five event. It's nicer to meet someone face to face, say hello in the flesh and start building some sort of relationship than to pick up the telephone and try cold-calling them.

If your blood runs cold in your veins and you get sweaty palms just thinking about going to an event on your own, then I hope I can convince you that it's worth it. Whether you're going to a small local event or a prestigious awards ceremony with heavy hitters in the room, the principles are the same — just start with hello. And that quite neatly brings me to how you should go about choosing the right events.

Choosing appropriate events

Ask yourself: 'Who do I want to talk to? Who do I want in or around my business? What sort of events do they attend?'

Typically, smaller businesses attend smaller local events. There may be an insurance representative, a lawyer, an accountant, a life coach, a massage therapist and a whole bunch of others, but they are generally smaller businesses. Now, if someone who represents your target market is in this room, you definitely need to attend. If, however, you want to talk to CEOs, managing directors and the like, they won't be at the smaller events. However, you may find them at a

Top 200 business awards gala dinner or similar events, so you need to find out what and where they are, get a ticket and be there too. Spend some time doing your research so that you don't waste time at the wrong place.

> ### Try this
>
> List all of the events you have access to and decide which ones you'd like to explore further.

Just because there is an event on near you, if your target market doesn't go there, it may be a waste of time to attend. That said, if you can go along even for a short while, you just never know who you may meet, as the previous case studies have shown us. You may not get a positive ROI on the day — it may be 12 months down the track — but one thing is for sure: if you don't go at all, you definitely won't meet anyone.

High-end events

It's worth looking at some of the higher end events. These may be full-on conferences such as the World Business Forum, which take place in major cities around the world each year. I was 'lucky' enough (I bought a ticket, booked a flight, took action) to go to this conference in New York, a city I had never visited before and a heck of a long way from Auckland, but it was worth the effort. Apart from the learning experience — listening to great speakers such as Bill Clinton, Seth Godin, Malcolm Gladwell and Jack Welch among others — the chance to meet these people and network with the other delegates at the event over breakfast, lunch and coffee breaks was enormous. By upgrading to a VIP ticket,

I was able to schmooze with business leaders from all around the world in small, designated areas away from the larger crowds and get a ringside seat up front in the first few rows so I didn't miss a thing. I would strongly recommend the event to anyone and will definitely go again.

So do some research. Find events that are perhaps not in your local vicinity, where you can take your networking and the people you meet up to another level. It could be well worth the extra effort.

Try this

Which events interest you that you will need to plan ahead to attend? They may even be abroad.

I recently went to a large business awards dinner event and found myself sitting next to one of the organisers of the event. After chatting for a while about who else was in the room, he pulled out a manila folder containing 800 bios—one for each and every businessperson in the room! He had certainly done his homework and knew not only the names of those at our table, but also their occupations and further background information. How much would you have paid to have that folder that night?

If you find yourself at a top business award dinner in your tuxedo, remember that the event is both business and after-hours social, so some shop talk is considered okay. It can be difficult to network beyond your table, depending on the event, so you may have to plan a little harder to create the opportunities you want. In the meantime, have you chatted to each person on your table?

Before you go

Now that you have found the event you want to attend, you need to do a little prep work so that you get the most from the event, and it's well worth doing.

What to wear

We do judge a book by its cover; everyone does, which means that your appearance is vitally important. While researching for this book, I came across an article on the website of great communications expert Carmine Gallo that talks very simply about how to dress for different business occasions. It was so simple, I felt there was no way I could explain it more clearly and make it my own, so full credit to Carmine. This is what she said:

> I met Matt Eversmann at a business conference. Eversmann was a US army ranger who fought in a battle in Mogadishu, Somalia, in 1993. The battle inspired a movie, Black Hawk Down. Backstage at the conference, Eversmann and I started talking about communication. 'What's the secret to great leadership?' I asked him. Eversmann said, 'Leadership starts from the moment you first meet a subordinate. Your whites should be whiter, your shoes should be shinier, and your pants should be better pressed. Always dress a little better than everyone else'.

There it is: 'Always dress a little better than everyone else'.

What he's saying is that by dressing 'a little better' you won't run into trouble by overdressing and trying to impress when it may not be appropriate. By dressing 'a little better' you've achieved your objective and are on safe ground. Let me give you an example.

If you're going to a business event at a design company where you know everyone will be in jeans and a T-shirt, you don't want to go in a full suit and tie; you'll simply look dumb and won't fit in. But that doesn't mean you can't 'dress a little better than everyone else', does it? Go in your suit pants, with a stylish open-neck dress shirt, and you will still look 'a little better than everyone else' without looking overdressed. Clean your shoes, press your clothes and if you are female, check your make-up. We have a couple of seconds to make the right impression, so don't make that impression the wrong one. You want to be remembered for the right reasons: 'the tall lady with the stunning shoes', 'the man with the great shirt'. You don't want to be remembered as the person with the creased suit and badly scuffed boots.

Take your business cards

You're going to need at least a handful of business cards, not two hundred. Hopefully you have a great-looking card, one that matches your brand and has all of your contact details on it, including your social media addresses. Use the back of your card as well: it's prime real estate. If no-one ever comments on how great your cards look, ditch them and get some better ones designed. They are part of your overall look. If you have to have corporate-issue ones, why not have some of your own personal ones printed that show your personality so that you can add your social media addresses to them and hand them out as well?

Have your own name badge

Even though you will more than likely be given a name badge when you get to an event, I like to use my own, which I had made for two reasons. (Remember Scott, the nametag guy?) Firstly, it has my logo on it as well as my name, and secondly it is magnetic so if I'm wearing a blouse, I'm not going to get nasty pinholes in it. They're not expensive to get made; just search online to find a supplier near you. Whether you're using your own name badge or attaching the one given to you, ladies, stick it high up on your lapel or blouse, away from your left boob! It can be a bit awkward to read for all concerned if it's lower down.

Grab your confidence

Confidence is obvious, if you wear it right. Walk tall, take your time, make good eye contact, have a firm handshake and smile. 'Express your pride through your stride' is a quote I heard recently, and a good one to remember. If you're not feeling at all confident, listen to some up-beat music before you walk into the event, or listen to a motivational podcast to get a quick lift up before you enter. Walk tall with confidence and watch who notices you arrive.

Rehearse your elevator pitch

There is heaps of information on writing your elevator or BBQ pitch, but it boils down to just a couple of things. What is the essence of what you do, and what is the slightly extended version of what you do? When someone asks what you do, what do you say? Two key areas to be aware of in this short piece of conversation are:

- *the first part* — may only be one, or two at the most, sentences long, but it describes what you do very simply (so simple a 10 year old would understand it)

- *the extended pitch* — includes a little more detail, such as your target market and location, for instance. It's not a free rein to spill out everything you can do for a possible client until they die of boredom or drift away.

Seth Godin has his own philosophy on what an elevator pitch should consist of. It is posted on his blog and is titled 'No-one ever bought anything on an elevator'. He begins by saying:

If your elevator pitch is a hyper-compressed, two-minute overview of your hopes, dreams and the thing you've been building for the last three years, you're doing everyone a disservice. I'll never be able to see the future through your eyes this quickly, and worse, if you've told me what I need to know to be able to easily say no, I'll say no.

He goes on to say that the best elevator pitch doesn't pitch a project but rather the meeting about a project and that it should be true, stunning and brief. It should 'leave the listener eager (no, desperate) to hear the rest of it. It's not a practised, polished turd of prose that pleases everyone on the board and your marketing team'. He also says elevator pitches should be about 'more conversations and fewer announcements'.

I find Seth Godin a man of great wisdom. He has a simple view and quite often states the obvious, but it's the obvious we can quite often be blind to. Until I read his blog post, I hadn't given this much thought, but he's right. Unless you pin them to the elevator wall, while you sell them your widget, no one is going to buy something from you in an elevator. But they do `buy' the interest. So sell the sizzle, not the steak.

When you get there

At most events, when you arrive there will be a table with all of the attendees' name badges laid out on it in alphabetic order and, even though you have your own perfectly branded name badge pinned to your lapel, it's a great place to hover and see the names of everyone else who is due to arrive. It's also a great place to loiter just for a moment so that you may meet someone else who is just arriving and you don't have to enter the room alone like Norman No Mates.

It can be a little awkward arriving on your own, but as you're there to meet other businesspeople, it forces you to chat to people you don't know rather than standing and chatting with the person from your office you came with—there's really not a lot of point to that.

Starting a conversation

The easiest way to start a conversation at an event is at the drinks table. As you pour yourself a cup of coffee or a glass of wine, ask the person behind you what they would like and, if they want the same as what you have just poured, give yours to them. This is not only a kind gesture, but it forces them to say something, usually 'thanks', and then the conversation has started between you. If you end up giving your drink away to someone who then walks off and leaves you, I would make a mental note not to waste my time trying to chat to them later!

So, you have your drink and you find yourself standing alone browsing the room. You need to make something happen or you may as well go home. Look around the room at the groups of people. You may find:

- larger groups of three or four people deep in a conversation, congregated around the person who is talking, everyone listening hard

- two people talking animatedly and gesticulating heavily, standing directly opposite each other

- two people standing shoulder to shoulder lightly chatting and taking in the room

- the lone ranger.

When it comes to making an approach to chat to someone, body language will tell you whether they will be receptive to you joining in their conversation. With the first example, the larger group of people, their body language is saying, 'do not disturb' as they are in a closed circle listening to the speaker. You may be able to approach them later, if they relax their stance.

The same goes for the second example as they are standing directly opposite each other, are deep in conversation with each other and are gesticulating wildly, perhaps having a heated discussion. Again, maybe you can approach them later, if they change their stance.

With the third example, their body language is very open. They are standing shoulder to shoulder and their body language is saying, 'we are open' so they are inviting someone to join them. In fact, they are positively encouraging you to join them, so go ahead.

The last example is a no brainer. This person is going to thank you for 'rescuing' them from being all alone, and will welcome you with open arms, so go ahead and approach them.

If you find yourself on your own, don't sulk or start playing with your smart phone, pretending to be reading emails and looking important. Put it away and make the effort or you may as well go home.

Knowing what to say

Firstly, just remember that most people in the room are as nervous as you are, and no-one wants to be left on their own, so the easiest way to get started is to find someone else on their own. They will be welcome and relieved that you initiated a conversation.

Starting a conversation with a complete stranger when you know absolutely nothing about them except that they attend the same networking events as you can be a bit daunting. But you need to make a start, so start with hello.

OAR-ation: remembering how to start a conversation

Just in case there is nothing obvious (or subtle) that you can use to make that opening comment, once you have started with hello, go straight to OAR-ation.

OAR-ation is an acronym that I use for remembering how to start a conversation when I encounter a complete stranger at an event. It's small and not overly clever and complicated, which makes it very easy to remember.

When you've opened with your greeting, what normally comes next: anything in particular or do you go blank? If you go blank, this is where you should think about OAR-ation:

- *O stands for occupation.* When you are at an event, nine times out of 10 the first question you will be asked is, 'What do you do for a living?' or 'What is your occupation?' so it makes sense to keep that consistent and not try to reinvent the wheel.

- *A stands for association.* How are you associated with the event? Are you a member, a guest of someone, the organiser? Find out what pulled you both to the same event. You may even have a mutual friend who invited you both so you have something in common straight off.

- *R stands for recreation.* Ask, 'What do you do in your down time? Are you a cyclist, a dancer, a cake decorator?' Find out what hobbies you may have in common that you can chat about. You don't necessarily want to talk shop all night, and shop talk may not even be that interesting to either party, but in order to get to know one another and keep the conversation going, you need to focus on something. If you don't ask the question, you also risk not finding out about something that you both really have in common and that may well bond you immediately, so mention your interests and find out theirs. Having a common interest definitely boosts the chances of a lasting relationship between two people.

In a perfect world, there would be another letter at the very beginning of OAR-ation, either a 'G' for greeting or an 'H' for hello, but they don't fit to make a memorable word and I would hope that starting with hello would be a given when you first strike up a conversation with anyone.

I once attended a wedding reception and found myself at a table that consisted of 'others'. We were not part of either party's family; we were the work colleagues and close acquaintances. After being seated, the lady on my right introduced herself by starting with hello, and promptly asked what I did for a living (Occupation).

Of course, our next question to each other was obvious: how did we know the bride or groom (Association)? Then, as we were at a lovely wedding on a Saturday afternoon, we skipped further shop talk and stayed with Recreation. A very short time later, we knew quite a few details about each other and, as my wedding-guest neighbour had no idea of my OAR-ation acronym, it proved to me that the OAR-ation method was indeed a natural way to create a conversation with a new acquaintance—and easy to remember as well.

Say their name

If you have ever read the great all-time classic *How to Win Friends and Influence People*, by Dale Carnegie, you will know some of his principles. He says that some of the key things to remember when it comes to meeting someone for the first time are:

- be genuinely interested in them
- smile

- use the person's name. It's the sweetest word in any language to them
- talk about their interests
- listen — get them to talk about themselves
- make them feel important but be sincere about it.

Remembering someone's name isn't so easy, for some reason, and if you're at an event where you're meeting quite a few new people, trying to remember them all is nearly impossible. Here's a trick to help you along:

Repeat their name a couple of times as soon as they have said it to you but in the context of the conversation. Then do it again later on.

For example, if you've just introduced yourself to Paul, the conversation may go something like this:

'Hi, I'm Linda Coles.'

'Hi Linda, I'm Paul Saunders.'

'Hi Paul. Good to meet you. So Paul, what is it that you do?'

And you're off. The key here is not to talk a whole lot about yourself, but ask questions of the person you have just met without it sounding like the Spanish Inquisition. People love to talk about themselves and so by asking Paul plenty of questions about his work or what his hobbies are, as long as it's done in a relaxed manner, you will be on safe ground.

When you've finished your conversation with Paul and you decide to leave or move off to chat with someone else, use his name again: 'Well, it's been great chatting to you Paul. There are a couple more people here today I need to chat to as well, so please excuse me.' By now, you should have remembered Paul's name.

Moving on to someone else

It's no good chatting to the same person all night unless you intend to go on a date! As most of us won't be planning that, it's useful to know how to politely move on to meet another person without offending the person you are talking to or leaving them on their own.

Continuing on from the example of Paul above, here are two things you could do:

- Introduce Paul to someone else before you move on. If there is someone in the room you know who would benefit from chatting to Paul, that's the best option. You can simply introduce Paul to this person with a sentence or two about what Paul does. You can then excuse yourself.

- You may need to simply move on if you don't know anyone you can introduce Paul to. So you can either excuse yourself by saying you need to refresh your drink, or to visit the bathroom. Paul may follow you to refresh his drink too, but people usually won't follow you to the bathroom.

Following up

When you return to your office, you really need to follow up with the people you spoke to at the event. So what's the best way to do that?

If there was a genuine interest and you both agreed at the event that a coffee catch-up another day was in order, pick up the telephone and give them a call to arrange the appointment.

If you had a connection but it's really not worth meeting again, then send a 'great to meet you' email that just has a simple 'thanks' message in it (not your sales patter). Or you may want to connect on LinkedIn.

Grant certainly benefited from following up on a chance encounter.

The right place at the right time

Grant found himself at a breakfast networking event early one morning that changed the course of his life forever.

It was Grant's final week as a creative director at a design agency so he went along to his local Business Network International (BNI) meeting. He very briefly got chatting to Richard who gave him his card and said, 'We need to talk further, but I have to go. Call me.'

Grant called Richard within a couple of days and they arranged a meeting—which also included another of Richard's contacts, Phil—about collaborating collectively and so making good use of each other's skills together. With Richard's search-engine optimisation skills, Grant's design skills and Phil's ability to build websites, between them they felt they had the perfect team to work together on several aspects of a client's project all at the same time.

As Grant was leaving his current employer anyway, he decided that he could just as easily work for himself as for another employer. So he decided to set up Waking Giants, a small design studio that concentrated on branding.

With his two new business acquaintances, Grant found himself working from one of their spare offices to get on his feet, and pitching with them for some deals with some great companies. In fact, in that first year he was introduced to many more key connections, became president of his local BNI, was introduced to the Entrepreneurs Organisation and shared nearly a quarter of a million dollars of revenue with his two business partners.

If Grant had never made it to that breakfast event and started talking to Richard, Waking Giants may never have been born and Grant may simply have moved on to work for someone else. Their relationship stemmed from being in the right place at the right time, and chatting to the right people. For Grant, the ROI for attending that particular event has been and continues to be in the hundreds of thousands of dollars—well worth the effort.

For Bruce it seemed that following up after making a connection at a networking event was not going to result in a successful collaboration.

Always follow up

Over a drink at a networking event of communications specialists Bruce met the communications manager of the local district health board and they swapped business cards. The next day Bruce emailed her to cement the connection and set out his skills and experience in case she ever needed a good PR consultant. She gracefully replied that, with their tight budgets, all their communications work was done in-house. It seemed like a dead end.

However, a week later she called Bruce with a 'you won't believe this but...' message. A large, urgent piece of work with a separate budget had crossed her desk and she had neither the capacity nor the time to complete the work to a high standard in the required time frame. They signed a contract and Bruce completed the work.

Once again, from Bruce making the initial contact— following up by email in this instance—a whole new contract and business relationship ensued. The ROI for Bruce ran into the thousands of dollars.

Following up with your new connections is vitally important no matter how you choose to do it.

Socialising with CEOs

Networking events are indeed a great place to meet people, but some would say they are simply filled with plenty of people who want to sell you something, and not very many of those who want to buy.

Many heavy hitters such as company CEOs do not frequent these events, so if CEOs are your target market, then you need to look elsewhere for them. Part III of this book will help you get in front of many CEOs in a digital format, but here we're just talking about networking freestyle.

CEOs don't frequent mainstream networking events for three reasons:

- They don't have the time.

- They know they will be sold to.

- They mix with similar level people at other functions such as board meetings of companies whose boards they sit on.

They also know that if they want to meet other CEOs they won't find them at these mainstream events, so they have to look at other ways of being introduced, such as through their connections or putting themselves in the right places— business class departure lounges at airports and the like— and networking freestyle. They have to be even more creative at putting themselves in the right place than the rest of us.

When in Rome...

Everything we've looked at so far has been written with a western focus, so it's worth mentioning at this point that there are very subtle differences—and in fact there can be very big differences—when greeting people from different parts of the world, in particular Asia.

The last thing you want to do is offend someone or, worse still, lose the deal because of something you did that offended your business acquaintance.

In Thailand, people do not greet each other by shaking hands. Instead, they simply put their hands together palm to palm and place them in front of their face. With their mouth closed, they bow slightly. It is quite all right to do exactly the same back when greeting them.

If you visit Malaysia, you'll find that while they greet each other by shaking hands, it's not nearly as strong a shake as you may know; it's much softer. That is not because they are weak, but because that's what they like. Once you have shaken hands, it is then customary to place your right hand on your heart.

The Japanese make more of a ceremony than most when exchanging business cards, which they call *meishi*. The business card should be pulled from a business card holder or leather case and the card must be presented facing upwards and towards the recipient, held with both hands at the corners, as this demonstrates respect. A business card is meant to be admired, so read it thoroughly; never just slot it into your pocket, and certainly never write on it, re-read it after you have put it away or deface it in any way. The best place to put it is back in your own leather card-holder case. Never give your card out 'playing card' style or stack your cards up for others to take one.

The Japanese also have another custom when doing business and that is *nominication*, which simply means drinking communication. You must go for dinner and drinks to get to know each other before business can be done. It is not considered an option, but an obligation.

Part summary

If only it was as easy for us to make new contacts and friends as it is for dogs and children—a quick hello and you're best buddies, off chatting and generally at ease with each other. Unfortunately, it's not that simple and we have to work at it. We have to put ourselves in the situation in the first place and take action, ploughing forward and starting with hello.

When we greet someone, possibly for the first time, our eye contact is vitally important as it tells the other person so much about us. The eyes are the window to our soul, and it's very difficult to fake our real feelings through our eyes. Unlike the rest of our body language, where we look and how we use our eyes when communicating can give up a lot of information about ourselves, both good and bad.

Try not to overdo your eye contact with someone; staring is very off-putting, making it hard for the other person to look elsewhere when they really want to. If you've caught someone's eye a couple of times and they have not acknowledged you, then don't force it; they're simply not interested in acknowledging or meeting you. You may want to practise with people you know well and get their feedback on how you make them feel.

Freestyle networking is a skill that takes a little practice to get right, but once you've mastered it, it can be extremely rewarding, both personally and financially. If you see someone you wish to say hello to, then have a plan in the back of your head. Make the first move, pass a comment, say hello, discover their occupation, steer the conversation, obtain their contact information and hopefully agree to follow up.

If you're attending networking events, and you should if only for a short amount of time, then go to the right events for you. If you are looking for CEOs as your target market, you'll need to look at bigger events, such as business awards and some of the larger conferences held worldwide. If your target markets are at your local chamber of commerce or BNI, then attend those. Dress 'just a little bit better' than the other people, grab your confidence and start by saying hello to whoever you meet. Don't think about selling your widget right now; you may not actually reap the rewards for a little while to come, but you have made contact.

Remember OAR-ation. It's the easy way to know what to say when you meet someone new. Start with hello, and then it's Occupation, Association and finally Recreation. You can't go far wrong getting others to talk about themselves, no matter what the event.

In a nutshell

- Make sure your eye contact is spot on: not too much and not too little. Our eyes are the windows to our soul.

- Go to your local networking events, even if your target market is not present. You just never know who you may meet. That meeting could change the way you do things or increase your bottom line.

- Freestyle networking is a great way to meet others away from the office environment, so take the opportunities when they arise.

- When you want to get to know someone, remember OAR-ation: Occupation, Association and Recreation, in that order.

Part III

How to build effective business relationships online

So you've met someone, exchanged business cards and you plan to make contact with them because you hope they will become a valuable business connection.

The most likely thing that will happen after you've gone your separate ways is that you will do a quick check online to see what Google has to say about this person (and probably their company too). Rest assured, if you're Googling them, they're probably Googling you. So, what will they find out about you? Are you web worthy and Google friendly?

Read the following chapters to learn how to:

- become web worthy
- get onto social networks
- mind your digital body language.

Chapter 9

Be web worthy

For many people, Google is the most important tool on the web.

Marissa Mayer

What would a new contact find if they Google you, and what can you find out about them?

Try this

Do a search right now for your name. If your name is easily misspelled, search for the misspelled version too and see what comes up.

There are a few things to note when you're doing a search:

- Are you on the first page or is it someone else with the same name? It can be confusing to someone who doesn't know you.

- Is there a photograph of you? This may simply be your avatar, the photo on your LinkedIn profile or maybe a conference photograph.

- Click on images within the search and see what pops up.

- Are there any photos of you with a glass of wine in your hand? It's easy to look like a drinker even if you're not, unfortunately.

- Is your company's website listed with your name?

- Are there any really great articles that come up that you have either written or are quoted in?

- Are there any articles that you would rather not be visible within the first couple of pages of results? Maybe you were part of a merger gone sour or an investment company that crashed.

Overall, are you happy about what you're projecting to others who are possibly looking you up online? If not, get some help.

Improving your profile

If you find search results about yourself that are not particularly favourable, you'll need to work hard and try to push them back a page or two by getting more and more good news about yourself on the top pages.

You'll need to get several good articles published by a well-known online site, either within your industry or, if it is newsworthy, a great news or blog site such as *The Huffington Post* or *The Business Review*, or a well-respected city news site such as *The Sydney Morning Herald*. As these sites are well ranked and well known, Google will automatically pull these posts to the early search results for your name. It's great credibility for your own personal brand at the same time. The best way to do this when you first start working on your personal brand is to use a PR company. PR companies don't come cheap, but in my experience it's money well spent to get the ball rolling. That, coupled with perhaps your blog pages, Twitter and LinkedIn, should see you just about right for some good search results of your name.

So what can you find out about your new connection? Apart from the obvious search results, have a good look through pages such as their LinkedIn profile. Is it complete or half finished? Is there any extra information in there, such as their hobbies? Maybe they sail at the weekend. This extra information is useful to have when it comes time to follow up. For example, finishing off your follow-up message with 'If you're sailing at the weekend, have fun' shows you have done a little homework and you are trying to be friendly as well as professional.

Show up online

Back in the very early '90s, the World Wide Web was born and it significantly changed the way we communicate. It enabled us to communicate and send documents to each other extremely quickly, rather than relying on what has become known as 'snail mail', and it scaled up how many people we could communicate to at the same time. Many of us suffer from email overload or 'email bankruptcy', which is where you just can't cope with any more emails, so you either delete the lot, or ignore them.

So where is this going? Well, I was going to write about how sending more emails to others will increase the chance of your name being seen in more places, but in the interests of the public's sanity, I won't. The fact that many countries have anti-spam laws to protect us from even more unwanted emails is another reason why I won't recommend it. However, I do strongly believe in having a great email signature that gets updated often.

Moving away from emails, the internet also gave us other ways of talking to more people across the globe easily—mainly forums, both open and closed. Auction sites, medical sites, interest groups and dating sites are just a few examples of forums and communities for discussing a common thread. There are now social networking sites specifically created for connecting and chatting around many different topics all in the one place, with the most common ones being Facebook for social activities with friends, and LinkedIn for business networking with connections. There are others, such as MySpace (which has recently relaunched itself), Instagram, Pinterest and a handful more. Each of these is quite different from the others; to survive, they need their own point of difference.

Social networking sites were born in the mid-2000s, with sites such as Facebook and LinkedIn being among the first and most popular ones. We will look at these now to see how you can use them to your benefit.

Facebook

Facebook is a great way of getting back in contact with people you've lost touch with — maybe from your school days or past employment — and also of keeping up to date with your current friends, relatives and even acquaintances if you so choose.

As we tend to post very short bursts of what we're doing or where we are, it's not the sort of information that we would feel the need to pick up the telephone to pass on. Taking a photograph of yourself and your partner at a game and putting it up on your Facebook page for the rest of your friends to see and comment on is far more practical than sending it in the mail.

If you're not yet on Facebook and have very little desire to be on there — being subjected to all the inane conversations and silly pictures may not be your cup of tea and may indeed be a waste of your time — consider that some of that inane conversation or those silly photos could reap rewards for you.

Keeping in touch with friends on Facebook who you wouldn't otherwise make the effort of contacting is a simple, easy and accepted way of doing things in the 21st century, so why not keep in touch and broaden your acquaintance base for your own enjoyment?

Never say never

Steve, a creative director at a design company, made the leap forward and succumbed to Facebook against his better judgement. 'I'm never going to join; it's a waste of time—wastebook, I call it.'

He reluctantly set his page up with an up-to-date profile picture, searched for a few friends, and reconnected with some old school buddies and some old work colleagues, which he actually found to be great fun. One of his old work colleagues accepted his friend request and immediately sent him a message asking for more information about what he was currently doing as a creative director, as she had just moved to a new job and they were looking for a company to work on their rebranding!

That was Steve's first taste of Facebook, and a business pitch was in the bag! Had he stuck with his 'never going to join, waste of time—wastebook' philosophy, he would never have reconnected with his old colleagues and would not have landed the work on their rebranding. For Steve the ROI for joining Facebook was a brand new contract.

Privacy settings

If you're worried about taking the plunge, then simply set your privacy settings to 'friends only' so that no-one who is not a confirmed friend of yours can see your personal page or the comments you make on friends' pages. The flip side of this is that you may want others to see you in order to give yourself maximum exposure and to 'virtually bump into' new people. You can of course turn on your 'follow' button, which allows anyone to follow what you have to say from your personal page, but you don't have to see their posts in your own news feed. They are not 'friends', only followers. This is a great way of exposing your own personal brand or building a relationship, albeit a little one-sided, with those who are interested in what you have to say. It's very much like Twitter, which gives a person the ability to follow you without you following them back. Being your personal page, if you're happy to share what you post there, or you're very careful what content you do put out, it's just another channel to utilise.

Networking on Facebook

I've met lots of great people and seen a less formal side to other connections by using Facebook in the way it was initially intended: for being social. With the 'follow' button available on many influential people's profiles, or their willingness to connect via a friend request, you're able to comment on their posts and let them and those watching know you exist. It's then up to you to add your thoughts and expertise to conversations, which you can do without looking like their new best friend. Ask yourself if you'd be doing the same thing offline as you're able to do online. Would it be considered too much? If the answer is no, then that's fine.

But it doesn't have to be all about adding your comment. Using the 'like' button is like leaving a few cents in a tipping jar. You're basically saying, 'Yes, I like' or 'Yes, I agree'. It lets the person who posted it know that you've heard it and appreciate the post, leaving a virtual tip.

So who would you like to get to know a little better or start networking with on Facebook? Make a list and then see if they have a Facebook presence. Has their 'follow' button been activated? Are they willing to accept your friend request? You may be surprised what you learn from them that is useful and it may be the start of a distant connection for the future. I'm not sure if tracking down your ex is a good idea though — that may cause a little trouble further down the track! We'll cover Facebook etiquette in chapter 10.

LinkedIn

LinkedIn is the most perfect place to meet other business people online as it's a database of more than 200 million people. While it's not yet in the same league as Facebook's one billion plus members, it consists of professional business-people looking to expose their brand and meet others online, with no-one enticing you to play virtual games such as Farmville. It's a serious online business forum.

Make sure you're set up correctly

When you're on LinkedIn, people will comes across your name or profile picture to check you out and find out a little more about you. This is your chance to shine and represent yourself well because LinkedIn is your own free personal business website containing your online boardroom of connections.

Spend some time getting a great head-and-shoulders photo, which is helpful for when you're meeting someone for the first time for a coffee as they will know what you look like. You're also several times more likely to come up in the search results if you have a photo.

Get your profile filled out fully and spend some time getting your summary written out well. This is the meaty bit that most people want to see. However, most people don't fill it out because it takes a bit of thinking about. In my view, it should contain what exactly it is that you do: maybe large projects you have worked on, what makes you tick and what sort of person you are.

You can read so much from a person's profile. If someone's profile is filled out but very brief in parts, they're either providing the bare minimum, or they just want to give you a high level of info and not the detail. If it's written in the third person ('Paul is...'), chances are they've copied it from their website or their PA has done it for them. If it's written in the first person ('I am...'), they have taken some care and put some thought into what they want you to read, and they want you to get a feeling for them from the tone they have used to write it. The latter is my preferred way of writing a profile. As we can't actually hear the person's voice when they speak, or see their eyes, we have to assume an awful lot, so writing it yourself helps towards our understanding of who you are.

Invite your database

Once your profile is all set, you can invite your email contacts and others to connect with you on LinkedIn. Make sure you do the profile before inviting everyone to find you on LinkedIn as the first thing your possible connection will do is look at your profile. Don't miss your chance to look great online.

Don't worry about who from your database you import at this stage as you'll be given the opportunity to select exactly who you want to send an invitation to when the list is uploaded.

Share some updates

Did you know that whatever you share in your update box, either on your profile page or on your home page, is seen by everyone you're connected to? It actually lands on their own homepage and that's where they see it. Not only that, but if they click 'like', 'share' or 'comment' on your update, the whole update appears on their direct connections home page as part of their own activity, so that means much more visibility for your post and your own brand. With that in mind, spend some time posting the right updates, things that you think your network will find interesting and you want to share or comment on. It all adds up to more exposure.

Join some groups

You'll need to join some networking groups as this is where you'll meet new people to possibly connect with who could become new clients or good business acquaintances. There are more than a million groups to choose from for all sorts of interests and industries, and the search functionality could definitely be improved so you may have to try different search terms to find what you're looking for. Groups come up in searches depending on what the group creator has put in the group title or group profile so if you're looking for medical appliances in the US, you may need to try both 'USA' and 'America' as separate searches to get what you're looking for. You can join up to 50 groups at any one time, but that would be a bit of a handful for you to effectively keep track of.

Let me share Tom's story about his experience of making something happen while taking part in a discussion in a LinkedIn group.

Tom's story

Being published in the *Harvard Business Review* is a great example of being in the right place at the right time and making something happen. I joined the *Harvard Business Review* group on LinkedIn as I liked receiving their cutting-edge information and wanted to become a contributor to *Harvard Business Review* one day.

After a year of reading the articles and discussions in the group, I stumbled across a post asking for specialists in the careers and personal development area to provide content. I immediately contacted the editor, pitched my article idea and then got the opportunity to write and be featured in the *Harvard Business Review*. If you could pick any university blog in the world to be published on, the *Harvard Business Review* would be right up there for most people and it was for me!

This led to me being positioned very well for a publishing opportunity with HarperCollins as well as supporting my successful application to go on an all expenses paid speaking tour around the South Pacific Ocean on a cruise liner.

I then leveraged this article by contacting *The Economist* magazine, pitching a new idea using the recent *Harvard Business Review* article as the credibility build. This then led to me being published and having my own Q&A forum for a week on www.economist.com in July 2012.

It doesn't take much to spend a little time in the groups and see what grabs your attention, and Tom's story is a great example of how things can snowball by taking the first step, reaching out and starting with hello. From the article in *The Economist* came a presenting opportunity, again through *The Economist*, and so the ROI for Tom, by networking and paying attention to what was being said in a LinkedIn group, has been extremely fruitful.

Joining groups not only allows you to start and take part in discussions, it also allows you to send a direct message to someone else in that group you wish to reach out to. This is where LinkedIn can really help you connect with people you may not ordinarily come into contact with anywhere in the world. Think about who you may like to message on LinkedIn and join the group that they're in. It's like being in the same room as them and wandering over to say hello, only it's virtual.

Use your connections

When it came to getting my first book published, I really wanted Wiley to be the publisher, but I had no clue how I was going to get my manuscript through to the right person to review. I really didn't want to send it through to the general email address and have it sit at the bottom of a pile. As it was coming up to the Christmas holiday period, I was hoping that someone would take it home with them and read it during a quiet moment. That was the plan anyway. But I didn't know anyone who worked there. However, I did know people who knew people who worked there!

I turned to my connections on LinkedIn to see who knew someone at Wiley. After a few quick emails to various connections asking if they could tell me the name of the person I needed to contact, bingo! I had the right person. I was then able to send my manuscript directly to them and the rest, as they say, is history. The book launched the following August, published by Wiley—mission accomplished! Could I have done that without my connections on LinkedIn? Definitely not. My own personal ROI for using LinkedIn in this way has been in the thousands of dollars and as Wiley is publishing this book too, it will continue to grow.

So how can you tap into those people you really want in or around your business, new clients and acquaintances?

Send a direct message

There are two ways of contacting people on LinkedIn, either via InMail or by direct message. You will need to have an upgraded or premium account to send an InMail, which is simply a private email through LinkedIn, but there is a cost for it (even though it's not much). The direct-message way is free, but it relies on the person you want to send a message to being in the same group as you. You can look at their profile to find out whether they are in the same group as you. If they're not, you simply join their group! Now you may be thinking, 'Hey, that's definitely stalking', but it really isn't. You're simply putting yourself in the same 'room' as the person you wish to chat to, except it's a virtual room. If I said to you that that person was right next door to the room you were physically in, would you stay put, or would you go and introduce yourself? It's exactly the same thing and as long as you're polite, then in either scenario, there really is no difference.

Find out who you both know

Whenever you view the profile of a person on LinkedIn who you're not directly connected to, you are able to see who you both know in common, or how you're connected. This is particularly useful when it comes to actually meeting or reaching out to this person via a message because you already have something or someone in common to break the ice. Let me give you an example. If I view Tom Peters's profile, I can see that we are both connected to Daniel Pink and Chris Brogan as these people are our shared connections, so I will bring either of these names into the conversation as a way of finding our commonality.

Writing your message

So what should you put in your message to make the best impression possible? If you're reaching out to this person for the very first time and you don't know them, keep your message brief and to the point—no more than 100 words, which is actually not very many so be specific. Add in your shared connection's name to create a link to how you 'know' them. Ask yourself what the main purpose or reason is for reaching out to them, and make that clear in your message. All too often, we receive messages that I really think equate to spam. They read along the lines of:

Hi Bill,

How are you today?

My name is Linda and I want to tell you about my company, Blue Banana, and how we can help you make more money...

Three hundreds words later...

I would love it if we could connect and chat more,

Linda Coles

Would you even read to the bottom of this message? I know I wouldn't. I'd delete it and I wouldn't bother to reply. If the sender thinks it's acceptable to send me such a message, I don't want to encourage them any further.

So keep it short and sweet. When you've finished writing it, ask yourself if you would be happy receiving it in your own inbox, or if it still comes across as too 'salesy'. Have you got to the point early on and made it clear what you're looking for? Have you used a great subject line to pique the reader's interest? Have you included a little bit of your personality in your message, or is it all corporate babble language?

Add to your message the fact that you have someone in common, particularly if the person you have in common has suggested you get in touch with the other person, because this can turn your message from a cold one to a warm one and will be received better. I discuss name-dropping in chapter 12.

Twitter

Twitter is a great way to come into contact with complete strangers from the safety of your own computer and, if you use Twitter as an icebreaker for a conversation starter, you can be quite strategic about it.

Suppose you particularly want to put yourself in the same space as one of your local business 'heroes' but you just don't mix in the same circles as they do. What choices do you have? You really would value this person's opinion on a project you're working on, so you could either:

- pick up the telephone and try to get past their gatekeeper
- send them a cold (unsolicited) email
- stalk them (not advised)
- write them a letter.

Or search for them on Twitter and follow their tweets.

At this stage, you simply want them to know you exist — that you're alive and well on this planet. Nothing more.

When your hero tweets, hopefully it's something that you can either re-tweet or, better yet, comment on. Now that particular tweet may be something quite mundane, such as a comment on their football team or the fact that their child is taking part in a local soccer derby this weekend. What you write really doesn't matter. What does matter is that you tweet back, and your comment may be something simple such as, 'Have fun. It was my kid's turn last weekend'.

It's not cyberstalking. Anyone who tweets publicly is putting themselves out there in the public eye. If you or anyone else chooses to comment on a tweet, that's fine because that's what Twitter is for: short conversations or pieces of content being shared by friends, colleagues and, more often than not, complete strangers. It's the perfect way to strike up a conversation with someone you may really want in or around your business in some way. Over time, you may find that something comes of the relationship and you meet up for coffee, but you will never know unless you try. One thing is for sure: if you don't make the effort and start with hello, they may never know you even exist.

I have nurtured relationships with prospects for long periods of time on Twitter, and we have giggled like teenagers when we've finally met up because we have already had a sort of 'online relationship' and we already know so much about each other and each other's businesses. Our relationship is already warm.

A lady who worked in advertising, Clarissa, tweeted that she loved some of the digital advertising that a certain sports team was doing. The sports team's digital head saw the tweet and thanked her via Twitter, and a conversation ensued which resulted in Clarissa's agency being asked to pitch for the account.

Blogging

You may not think blogging can be a place to network and meet others online, but it is. When you visit a blog regularly over time, you may want to leave your comments about your thoughts and experiences rather than just reading the post and carrying on to the next thing. If you are a regular visitor to that particular blog, you may notice that there are others who regularly leave useful comments, so by leaving your comment you're adding to the online conversation as most blogs give you the option to be notified when other people make comments too.

As you have to sign in using software such as Disqus to leave your comments, your online avatar or photo will appear and this is another great way to show off your personal brand.

The reasons for adding your comments to blogs are twofold. First, you're showing your appreciation of the author's post, and you're either leaving a positive comment or challenging them on their thinking with a different type of comment.

Second, more people can see that you exist because, up until they read your comment, they had no idea. You have only just surfaced into their world.

So if leaving comments enables others to 'meet you' virtually, then the same applies to you being able to meet others virtually. With that in mind, if you'd like to get on the radar of a certain CEO, find out if they write a blog that you can visit. What a great way to start getting your name known to this person, particularly if your comments are all positive or constructive ones.

People who keep a blog invariably like to see a written response, both good or challenging comments, but no-one likes to receive an outright rude one and there really is no need. Just because you're not there in person to say what you're about to say doesn't mean you can hide behind your computer and a certain amount of anonymity and write rude comments online.

The other thing to remember when writing a comment is that any other blog visitors can see it and it's your own personal brand on show. So give your comments a good deal of thought before you hit 'post' and make sure your own brand is shining in the right light.

~

There are so many ways you can network effectively online and I have explained the best ways here. The important thing to remember is that you need to be as natural and friendly online as you are offline.

Chapter 10

Digital etiquette and body language

I speak two languages, Body and English.

Mae West

For some strange reason we simply don't behave the same way online as we do offline. Online our manners and personality go straight out the window—it's almost as if we're talking computer to computer rather than person to person. After all, it is a real person sitting behind the computer, a person with feelings and a brain. So unless you're someone with a personality disorder, or are naturally rude, just be yourself and you won't go far wrong.

When communicating via computer using email, newsletter or any of the social sites, we still need to convey our personality, our humility and our authenticity just as we do in a face-to-face conversation. Without facial expression, eyes to read and tone of voice to listen to, we could be in danger that the receiver of our message reads something quite different from what we actually intended for them to read. So how can we put some real etiquette in place so that we don't mess up and give the wrong impression about ourselves when we network and connect with others online?

Using LinkedIn

There are some really simple features on LinkedIn that get brushed over with no thought when we could use them to make the whole experience so much better. Think about when you send a connection request to someone. Do you just send the pre-populated request template that LinkedIn gives you, which states, 'I'd like to add you to my professional network on LinkedIn', or do you take this opportunity to personalise your request with a message such as, 'It was great to meet you yesterday. I'd like to add you to my professional network on LinkedIn and keep in contact with you'? This is one of your chances to show your personality and connect at the same time, so make sure that the tone and content of your message are a true likeness of how you would speak to the person if they were right there next to you.

Think also about what you do when someone sends you a connection request and you want to accept or decline it. If you choose to accept it, then don't just click 'accept' and move on to the next thing you want to do. Take a moment to click on the sender's name and check out their profile. In doing this, you're simply looking to find out a little more about your new connection, whether it is where they have worked in the past, their current position or people you may have in common; just find a little more detail. Once you've done this, send them a quick message to say thank you for connecting and whatever it is you wish to mention that you found in their profile. Follow this up with your offer to help in any way, if that's applicable and authentic to you.

If you were at an offline networking event and someone came up to you and said 'hello', you wouldn't just say 'hello' right back and walk off, would you? You'd stay and chat for a while. Well it's just the same online, so you need to make that little extra effort, as though you were communicating face to face.

Using Twitter

I wanted to include Twitter in here because Twitter is not like any of the other social sites; it's quite unique. So what should you be aware of on Twitter so that you don't get it wrong and offend anyone?

Here are a few suggestions to consider:

- By all means send a welcome DM (direct message), but an automated 'salesy' one? No!

- Do reply to as many @replys as you can. They are, after all, talking to you and they deserve a response.

- Don't feel the need to thank everyone who gives you a #FF—it can simply be too much.

- Remember, everyone can see your controversial conversation, your risky photos or your explicit language; it's all public and searchable.

- Use the sender's name when you reply, particularly the first time. People love to hear their name.

- Don't fill your Twitter stream up with too many #tags in each post. Save some space so others can RT (re-tweet) your tweet.

Most Twitter accounts are quite 'faceless' in that you can see the person's username quite clearly, but very often you don't know the actual name of the person tweeting from the account. This is particularly common with brands. Make sure you have a name included in your profile so that when you follow or chat with someone they can find out a little bit more about you and greet you with your name. Remember Dale Carnegie's principle stating that you should use people's names? It's an important part of connecting.

Using Facebook

With some people choosing to have their Facebook privacy settings wide open, there can be plenty of their life on show across the internet, which, depending on your view, can be a good or a bad thing.

From an online networking point of view, if they're happy to expose their interests and home life, that will give you some great background information on them when it comes to finding out more for building up an online or offline rapport. Just as you would do a Google search for someone before meeting them, looking for a snippet of information on their Facebook page can be very useful. They're in control of what they post; you just need to be clever and use it. Imagine going into your meeting for the first time knowing that you both have a keen interest in road cycling and that your new contact is going over to watch the Tour de France next year? Awesome intel, and a great way to break the ice and get to know one another.

What is important to remember here is that you're not in any way being a stalker. You're not trying to get into their private life, which they have perhaps kept private, and you're not a private detective either—just a smart person doing their best to get to know someone a little better for a business advantage. If the information is freely available, why not use it? If the information shouldn't be out there, it shouldn't have been posted in the first place and the person you're looking up is usually the one in control of that.

From an etiquette point of view, you may very well be tempted to send a friend request to certain people you've strategically picked out as potential business connections...but beware. Remember that LinkedIn is your boardroom of connections and that Facebook is your coffee shop and that very different conversations and etiquette take place in each social media site. For that reason, if you've tried to get in contact with a possible business connection, say the editor-in-chief at *The Harvard Business Review,* and you haven't been successful through your other business channels and tools including LinkedIn, it's really not polite or good form to try to 'friend' them on Facebook or send them a business message through Facebook. I have seen requests by people on popular websites asking various team members not to do this. But while it obviously goes on, it's really not cool.

When you do view or follow someone's Facebook page, you may be able to see who their friends are by the comments they leave on various posts. Don't be tempted to 'friend' any of these people in the hope that they will mention your name or pass a message on to your original 'target', for want of a better word. That's even less cool. I saw this happen only recently, and the person who was on the receiving end was mighty annoyed. That to me is just a bit too much like being a 'social stalker'. Here's an example to show you what I mean.

Phillip's story

Joe, a candidate for a job, connected with me in the hopes of gaining access to our hiring manager. I did know the hiring manager, but didn't know Joe. As we were connected he asked me to make a recommendation on his behalf and introduce him to the hiring manager. I had never even met Joe, and certainly had no background or knowledge of him, so I refused to do so.

I felt as though I was being used—connected with solely for the purpose of someone and their own agenda. We disconnected shortly after that.

I can't imagine anyone not being as annoyed as Phillip in a situation such as this one.

Posting from your business page onto another business page is absolutely fine. It drives more traffic to your page when others see your comments and your page name attached to them, as long as your comments are relevant to the discussion taking place.

An etiquette breach that irritates a lot of page administrators is when people leave comments and then post links to their own sites at the same time. This is particularly prevalent on very busy Facebook pages where many comment streams are generated, so those who think this is good practice have a captive audience to see their links. Personally, if I were the administrator of the page, I would delete them and politely ask the offending person to stop doing it and, if they carried on, then block and report them to Facebook as it equates to spam and cheap tricks, after all.

When you come across something worth sharing on another person's page or profile, don't be tempted to save that content and make it your own for a later post. Use the 'share' button that Facebook provides for that very purpose so that the originator of the post gets recognition. Share it if it's worth sharing, but be truthful about its origin.

Here are some other etiquette reminders on what not to do when using Facebook:

- Don't use lots of exclamation marks to get your point across!!!!!!!!!!

- Don't complain about work and co-workers, some of whom you may be 'friends' with.

- Don't use #tags in conversations that are not on Twitter. They don't work anywhere else and don't make sense to the rest of the conversation.

- Don't tell your Facebook 'friends' that you're having a culling session, so that if they don't see any more of your posts, they won't think they were culled.

- Don't use CAPITAL LETTERS. Are you shouting digitally? It's not needed; we can read lower case just fine.

Newsletters

Yes, there is etiquette involved when sending newsletters out to your database.

Think about what you currently put in your newsletter. I bet it contains information about some or all of the following:

- an office move

- an announcement that a new team member has joined

- your latest offer or deal

- an industry news item.

And that's about it. It will usually be written by the marketing department so the 'corporate' voice will come across, even if you're not a corporate-style company. Nonetheless, it will lack any real humility as well as any content that is really useful. Now this is not a lesson on how to market your business through email marketing, but if you want your newsletter to be well read, well shared and well worthwhile, you'll need to make sure you have included a few things:

- an appropriate greeting including the receiver's name

- appealing content

- appropriate and authentic language and tone

- images where possible

- an option to unsubscribe easily.

You want anything you do online to be shared around and to get exposure to those new eyeballs, to get your business or personal brand out there making new acquaintances as much as possible. But you also want to generate a great reputation as you go, which is why it's important that you do the job right.

An appropriate greeting can be anything from a simple 'hi' or 'hello' to a more formal 'good morning', followed by a name. The most important part to remember here is to use their name. Remember Dale Carnegie's words: 'a person's name is to that person the sweetest and most important sound in any language'. So use names as often as you can without going over the top. That means starting your newsletter with their name, and even starting your last paragraph with their name before you sign off. An example may read: 'So [insert name] we look forward to...' Having their name right before you sign off will give even more of a personal touch, and just like when someone uses your name to address you, they will instantly take more notice.

Content that appeals is the right way to give your readers what they want and what they want to share.

Try this

Ask yourself, 'What is the biggest frustration, problem, need or desire of the person receiving my message?' That's what your content should focus on.

If you're a software company, your newsletter could contain quick training tips on using your product, news articles on product development and maybe a training video. Thinking back to your customer's problem, need or desire, this would be far more useful than what you may be currently sending out.

Quick tips are a great way to get your content shared with others too. For example, if you're in real estate and you're sending a newsletter out with just your new 'For sale' listings on it, it may be a bit dull. If you then add in some house-selling tips, it becomes useful information that the receiver may well pass onto their friends, who may just happen to be trying to sell their home.

Appropriate language and tone can be tough to get right. I recently received a newsletter from a company and was a little surprised to see the amount of swear words in there. Now while they were only moderately bad words, it still made me think they had gone too far. On the other hand, were they simply being authentic? Maybe that's how they speak to each other around the office and to their customers directly. Maybe I wasn't their target market, and a different generation may have thought it was okay, but their tone and language definitely did nothing for me to want to share it.

Images are fast becoming known as the way to get your message shared more. If you spend time on getting the right image for your story, make sure you put your company web address alongside your message. That way, when it does get shared, others know where it came from and can visit your website to find out more. Don't be tempted to steal images off the internet. Invest a few dollars and get them from sites such as www.shutterstock.com or www.istockphoto.com.

Unsubscribing should be simple. While you don't want to see someone go, be gracious about it and accept that sometimes what you're peddling is just not relevant to them anymore.

Lastly, if you're going to export your connections' details from LinkedIn and import them into your newsletter database, ask them for permission first. Those connections have agreed to connect with you on LinkedIn. However, they didn't sign up for your newsletter and you may find you annoy a few people by sending them unwanted mail.

Say, for example, you're a software company and I'm a florist. If you've added me to your newsletter database, even though the product or service you're pushing isn't relevant to me, I may not only unsubscribe, I may also 'unconnect' from you on LinkedIn.

Your digital body language

When you meet someone in person, you form an opinion of them within just a few seconds—rightly or wrongly, we all do it. Face to face, that person doesn't have a great deal of control over your opinion, except for in the way they greet you and the way they present themselves. But online, you can hide or flaunt yourself in many different ways, so sometimes it can be hard to 'get a feel' for a person when all you have to go on is a LinkedIn profile and an email message.

Text talk

The way you write an email or a profile of yourself is a dead giveaway of your generation. It wouldn't occur to me to write the way we do in a text message when writing an email or a status update, but for someone under 20, it's the norm. So, for example, stay away from 'lol' if you're emailing. It doesn't look professional and won't do you any favours.

Capital letters

Using all capital letters is the digital body language equivalent of shouting. Writing with capital letters online doesn't make your voice any louder, but it does portray your anger and frustration big time and is not appropriate.

Exclamation marks and ellipses

It's okay to use exclamation marks when you want to show a little passion or anger, but beware, overuse could make you look like you're permanently angry or aggressive! 'Have a great weekend!' is simply adding in that you really hope they do have a good one, but if you were to write 'I'm glad it's the weekend!!!!' to your boss, it could be taken as 'Yeah, it's going to be a great weekend', or 'I hate working here. I'm glad it's the weekend'.

It's the same when you use ellipses...What are you trying to say? For example, starting with 'Linda,...' sounds to me like I'm going to get a dressing down, and 'Linda, how are you doing with that report...?' really means, 'Where the heck is it?'

Smiley faces

Adding smiley faces is an easy way of making sure that the receiver of your message takes what you have written in a relaxed manner, particularly if there could be two ways of understanding something. Some people are of the view that smiley faces are not professional and should be avoided, but I think if it fits with your personality, then why not? If you're unsure how your message might be received, rather than risk the receiver getting the wrong end of the stick, pick up the telephone or pay them a visit; it's not only safer, it's a better form of communication. Emails are used far too much in my opinion, but are great if you need to keep a written record of a conversation or include others in it.

Spelling

Some internet browsers, such as Firefox, already have a spell checker built in, so no matter where you fill something in online, you will be alerted if you make a spelling error. It's really easy to write letters in the wrong order in a word. Spell check will correct these sorts of errors. Spelling errors will make your online contribution to groups, forums and discussions look sloppy and, again, people will make a judgement about you, so it's worth getting your spelling right.

Online images

If you're going to be meeting new connections offline in a coffee shop or at your office, for example, then it's helpful to keep a current and professional photograph on sites such as your LinkedIn profile and your company website. The thing here is to keep it current. So a special mention to those who are still using a photo from 10 years ago: get it updated.

You may have had a professional photo taken in the past—perhaps a glamour shot, taken in a studio and then touched up. This is great for the mantelpiece at home, but the arty black-and-white glamour shot has no place as your LinkedIn profile picture. We want to see what you look like—what you really look like—so we know who you are when we finally meet you. Keep it real and authentically you. If you change your hairstyle regularly, you will need to change your gravatar (globally recognised avatar) too.

Greetings and sign-offs

Online forums and discussion groups are all very public, with lots of people watching what's being said and not contributing at all. (I call them the 'web watchers'.) They're everywhere, and just because they don't make themselves known by leaving a comment doesn't mean they're not interested in your personal or business brand, or what you have to say.

You're totally in control of how you conduct yourself in these forums and groups, and you have the choice of only showing a side of you that you want people to see, or the whole 'lock, stock and barrel' you.

Going back to the point I made earlier about using a person's name where you can, it's the same for all groups and forums—in fact, everywhere you connect. Consider starting your comment with a salutation such as 'hello' followed by the person's name, and finish with a valediction such as 'regards' at the end of your comment, just as you would in any written conversation. Again, it's just good manners to do so.

You may think it's a bit over the top and a bit too formal, but because of the way we communicate so openly online, and the fact that there's usually a time delay before a response, it matters. If you're having a real-time conversation with someone, after the initial post you can probably drop the formality, just as you would if you were having a conversation back and forth via email or in person. But if you're catching up on some comments that need responding to, it needs to be the real deal.

~

In doing research for this book, I used my social channels to find out what annoyed people from an etiquette point of view. One person actually said etiquette wasn't really that important, 'so pull up your big-boy pants and get over it'.

We sometimes get door-to-door sales-people such as the Avon lady knocking on our door without announcing themselves first. Were they not the equivalent of the spam we deal with now? Are they not unwanted interruptions trying to sell us something? They lacked etiquette by knocking on our door, right?

I'll leave that for you to decide, but I think there's no excuse—whatever the situation—for bad manners when dealing with another human being. Virtually or in person, etiquette is important.

Chapter 11

Don't forget the telephone

My sole inspiration is a telephone call from a director.

Cole Porter

It's so easy to simply email or text someone and have a conversation that way rather than picking up the phone and actually talking. By communicating using either of these mediums, we may be limiting the chances of experiencing serendipitous moments that may be hovering nearby and that we may not otherwise be aware of. By having a brief text conversation, or dropping someone a reply to their email, we could be missing out on opportunities. But, of course, it's easier to reply to a message in either of these two mediums and then quickly move on, back to the main task at hand.

When you get an enquiry via email from a potential new client, what do you do? Do you answer it and then file it in your 'new enquiry' file and perhaps follow up the next week? Or do you pick up the telephone and call your potential new prospect and have a chat? I bet most people would go with the first option, particularly if the email from your new prospect is a simple price enquiry that you can deal with easily. After all, you get heaps of those enquiries don't you? So why waste your time replying by telephone?

Only recently I picked up the telephone to respond to a new enquiry and the gentleman on the other end of the phone actually thanked me for taking the time and trouble to respond to his enquiry and said that it was refreshing, not to mention nice, to have had a personal response. To me, that just highlights that we have begun to rely on these other forms of electronic communication far too much, which isn't necessarily right. You can quite easily stand out from your competition just by bringing back the human touch; it's just not so common anymore.

By picking up the telephone, you're allowing yourself to find out a little more about your new prospect, and so you're able to build more of a relationship, which can only be a good thing, whether now or in the future. The tone of their voice, the snippets of information you can pick up and the chance to make a new acquaintance all add up to staying human in a technology-mad world.

Douglas found that talking to a persistent telephone caller really changed his life. He tells his story.

Douglas's story

If that's that guy phoning back again, I'm hanging up, I said to myself.

'Hello.'

'Hello. I know I've been phoning you frequently but if you let me explain why, it will be worthwhile for you.'

So began a friendship and business venture that's lasted 20 years. The call was to enrol me in an NLP (neuro-linguistic programming) practitioner's course and the person making the call was to become one of my two closest friends and business partner to this day. The other one? Well, they were in the program as well.

At first we were just a bunch of strangers brought together for a few months by some excellent salesmanship and a keenness to learn something, or maybe it was just to stop the bells—the ringing of the persistent phone calls. (And yes, in those days the phones did actually ring!)

As usually happens among a group of 20 or so people brought together for a prolonged period of time, mini groups formed. The 'jokers' and 'boundary pushers' (well, okay, troublemakers), the more studious ones, the quiet learners... we were all there and, as a large group, I'd like to think we were considerate and supportive of each other.

My mini group was predominantly made up of the 'jokers' and the 'boundary pushers'. We were keen to learn and to find shortcuts to getting the most from the program. Most of us had business backgrounds and we had some heavy hitters in the party department, resulting in our home study and exercise practice sessions often taking place in various bars and on a variety of dance floors.

As the program developed I often found myself in conversation with two particular people in our group. As egos were allowed to slip, conversations got more meaningful and interesting connections began to develop. Common questions and areas of curiosity among the three of us began to surface. The motivation to answer those questions and satisfy our curiosity became what has so far been a lasting foundation for our friendship and business focus, which has stood up to a few severe tests over our time together.

Other people from the program kept popping up over the years, from one of New Zealand's great volunteer sporting organisers to a mate of my daughter's—both powerhouses behind our five-a-side soccer success for many years.

(continued)

> ## Douglas's story *(cont'd)*
>
> For me, enrolling in the NLP program was certainly a serendipitous event in my life and, on reflection, a reminder that sometimes it pays to answer the phone and listen to what the caller has to say.

Wow—a life-changing ROI from picking up the phone and saying hello! Douglas listened to the caller and it changed his life. I wonder how many calls we've missed or not listened to because of a perceived or actual pushy salesperson on the other end?

The other great thing about picking up the telephone is that you're less likely to misconstrue something, which is always a risk with emails. Unless you add smiley faces to your emails, how else can you ensure that what you've intended to say is what the reader actually reads, or if you're wanting to be a bit more hard-nosed with someone, that they get the message? That said, there is certainly a place for email.

Don't forget email totally

Sometimes, you just have to use your email, particularly if you need to keep a record of a conversation so it can be filed, or if you want to make an enquiry about something yourself, such as a holiday booking. If you do use email, I'm a great believer in having an interesting email signature with links to your social pages and website so that the person you're emailing can click on the links to find out a little more about what you do, should they so wish. You never know who they may forward your emails to.

After I booked a holiday home for an Easter long weekend break by email some time ago, the holiday home owner got in touch to arrange to meet me for a coffee beforehand as he had seen from my signature what I did for a living and he wanted to see if I could help his business. Without a full email signature, with all of my information a click or two away, he would never have known what my business was about and that he needed it. The ROI on my email signature more than covered my weekend break booking, and I have since been back several more times.

You just never know where your email may end up if someone forwards it on to their friends and colleagues. This is exactly why Vanessa ended up attending an event that changed her life.

The birth of Venus

Vanessa received a random email several years ago about a networking event at the local yacht club. The subject of the email was 'Conscious evolution'. Wondering what on earth that was, she decided to go along and find out more. Something seemed to be tugging at her.

The speaker talked about having dreams, how we must fulfil our dreams and that having a dream was a sign to go on and make something happen and create our life around whatever it is that lights us up.

At the end of the talk, Vanessa went up to the presenter and thanked her for the inspiration she had given her, saying that she felt compelled to do something for female entrepreneurs and start a network of support. The speaker replied with a question: 'So when are you starting?' That was the trigger she needed to get on and do it. The following week, Venus was born and it is still going strong today.

Had Vanessa never responded to the email that landed in her inbox, she may never have pursued her dream and started a female entrepreneurs support group. The ROI for Vanessa was life changing and financially rewarding.

~

You can meet people in the funniest of places and it doesn't always have to be in person. Anytime you have the opportunity to chat to someone, whether it be on the telephone, via email or in any other manner, do so — you just don't know where that conversation could lead you.

Part summary

When you've finally met your new connection, you're both more than likely going to Google each other to find out more, but do you look great online? Are you web worthy? What do you need to do to make sure that when someone searches for you something really great comes up, including an impressive LinkedIn profile? You may need the help of a PR firm to get the ball rolling for you by getting any articles you've written placed on prominent news websites.

Use the social networks to build relationships as well as to network with others. At the very least, as someone in business, spend some time on LinkedIn. Don't think of this time as playing or surfing. You're networking so it's definitely part of your marketing strategy and shouldn't be avoided. Even with Facebook, if you're networking with strategic contacts—putting yourself on their radar, showing them you're alive and well on this planet—then it's time well spent.

Remember that blogs and leaving comments on blogs too will expose your brand to others, particularly if there's a regular readership for you to interact with. You never know, if your comments are regular and thought provoking, you may get asked to write a piece or someone may ask for your opinion to be included in a bigger article.

Just because you're talking from behind a computer and not in person, don't let your etiquette slip. Good manners are still important, particularly if you're having a conversation over extended time periods or zones.

Always use a person's name in a greeting, whether you're chatting on Twitter or more formally on LinkedIn. A person's name is extremely important to that person.

Never forget the good old-fashioned telephone. We rely far too much on replying to a new enquiry electronically. Then it's dealt with, filed away and possibly forgotten. Pick up the phone and start with hello. The chance to start chatting in person to another complete stranger is an opportunity, not an interruption.

In a nutshell

- Get web worthy. Become active about looking great in the search results for your name.

- Use the social networks, particularly LinkedIn, for networking online.

- Remember your digital manners. Manners count online too.

- Pick up your telephone and call when you can. It's an opportunity, not an interruption.

- Make sure you have a full and attractive email signature. You never know where your emails may be redirected.

Part IV

How to understand and leverage behavioural styles

We've looked at networking freestyle at events as well as online and we've discovered a few places where you can meet new people and start with hello. As with many aspects of your business, building a good connection base needs to start with a strategy or plan so that your efforts can be measured when you reach your end point. If you don't know what or who you're trying to reach, you won't know if you've been successful or not.

Read the following chapters to learn:

- how to create a strategy for expanding your business connections
- who or what you can leverage to make new connections
- who you're talking to by assessing their behavioural profile.

Chapter 12

Create a strategy

Strategy is straightforward—just pick a general direction and implement like hell.

Jack Welch

In order to expand your business connections by talking to more strangers, you'll need a strategy. Strategy can be a scary word, but don't get too hung up on it. It doesn't need to be a 10-page document, just a general direction with an end point and actions to get there. If you break into a cold sweat just thinking about devising a strategy, then simply change the word 'strategy' to 'plan'; it works just the same.

Great lawyers hit the courtroom with a strategy or plan already in mind because if they don't, they will undoubtedly fail. They know which direction they want to take a witness in, and which questions and answers will get them there. This in turn will steer the direction of the jury and hopefully produce the verdict they want.

A football game is just the same. Coaches and managers will devise a strategy before the season starts and then for each game before they kick off. They will also alter their strategy on the hoof if the game fails to go in the direction they want it to. There's no point in leaving it until the end when it's too late.

A pilot follows a charted course to get to their destination safely and on time, but if an incident occurs or adverse weather conditions arise, they will need to alter their course to arrive at their destination safely, albeit a bit late.

Your efforts to build a great connection base are no different.

You'll need two strategies: one for your offline networking in face-to-face situations, and also one for your online networking. They need not be too far removed from one another but, as each way of networking is slightly different, the two sets of actions required to get you to your end point will be quite different.

Determine your end point

The first part of devising your strategy is to decide what your end point or goal is going to be. Is it to be connected to a particular person or persons, to do business with a particular company, to become world famous at something or just to grow your business connections or followers? Whatever it is, write it down. Now you have your end point. All you have to do now is work out how to get there.

Let's say you want to meet with the CEO of your national airline — so you now have your end goal. Where will you find this person? As CEO, you probably won't find them at the smaller networking events so you're going to have to think bigger. As CEO of a national company, do they present at conferences, attend big business award functions or fly often? Airport lounges, particularly those with designated business travel lounges, are good places to bump into other business-people. If these are the places you may need to go to in order to have a chance at meeting the person you want to bump into, then follow the eight principles we talked about in chapter 7 of this book.

Show up in person

I'm not suggesting you spend all day in an airport lounge looking for new prospects or hoping to chat to your hero, but when you're travelling, be alert to who is around you and how you can start a conversation with them. Likewise, be on the lookout at conferences and seminars and if your opportunity is there, position yourself to be able to start that conversation.

If the person is presenting at the conference, don't attempt to chat before they have given their presentation. They won't thank you for it and you will have more success if you wait until afterwards. Beforehand, they will be mentally fixating on their speech and nothing else; so don't interrupt their train of thought. When you do wait until after they've presented, you can easily start chatting about how useful you found their speech, and what you will do because of it. Most speakers like to feel that they are helping to change the world and making a difference somewhere, no matter how small, so take advantage of this piece of knowledge.

Show up online

You'll also probably find them online, as any switched-on businessperson will have at least a LinkedIn profile. They may also have a Facebook or Twitter account, and even a blog.

You'll need to make a list of the people you wish to make contact with, as this list could be quite different from your offline list. There are people in the business world you would never come across in person because they live on a different continent. Using online tools is an easy and cost-effective way of making contact.

Once you have your list of people, search for them on LinkedIn as this is the most obvious place for them to show up online. When you find their profile, have a look to see if you have anyone in common and what groups they are a member of. Remember that you can send a direct message to anyone on LinkedIn who shares a group with you, free of charge. It's not made very obvious but the facility is there, so go to the group your prospect is in, search for their name and you'll find the facility for messaging them on the right-hand side of the screen. You could also use the InMail service, which is part of the premium account. Either way, there are not many people on LinkedIn you can't get a message to directly.

Make your message stand out

Your message to your online prospect needs to be very similar to what you would say if you were networking freestyle. Begin by finding something in common. Don't be tempted to send a note full of sales patter or, even worse, an over-the-top message about how amazing you think the person is and how you'd love to connect. Sure, tell them why you're contacting them, but keep it brief, to the point (less than 100 words) and finish it off with a great subject line and a final sentence containing something that will catch their eye.

Let me give you an example. I was at a press conference and at the end I wanted to make contact with one of the main reporters regarding an event I was holding later in the year. As they were all very much focused on reporting the current event and getting their own story straight for their live report back, there was no opportunity to speak to him. So near and yet so far! So I had to bide my time and follow up online afterwards. I sent him an InMail—which was the only option open to me as he wasn't in any groups—briefly said what I was contacting him for and followed up the last sentence by saying, 'Loved the rebel green socks with your suit yesterday. Nice touch.' I also added a subject line of 'Green socks', which I thought should catch his eye. My aim here was to make him smile at the end of my message, making him more inclined to reply back with a favourable response. This works for me because of my style and behavioural profile (I discuss behavioural profiles in chapter 13) but it may not work for everyone.

Within a few minutes, he responded favourably with his phone number and direct email address and also the offer of pitching the event to other television shows as well. At the end of his message, he wrote, 'I love bright socks ha ha'. My message had resonated with him; now I just had to organise the next step.

Try this

Once you've made your list of online people who interest you in some way, send them your message or a tweet and wait for their response.

Following up from a meeting in person

Without the follow-up, you may just have been wasting your time, so this part is crucial and is the part that frequently gets left out. We've probably all been guilty of not following up, thinking it's too hard, or thinking our new connection won't remember us. Or we may just be plain scared of the rejection that could follow. I urge you to bite the bullet and do it. Hopefully you'll be pleasantly surprised and, if you got on very well initially, they will be pleased to hear from you again. Try following up by telephone first, but if they don't answer, never leave a message. If you leave a message, you're relying on them calling you back and if they have a hectic schedule at that time they probably won't call. If you follow up again after you've left a message that they haven't responded to, you may look a bit desperate.

Following up from a virtual message

It's much harder to follow up from a virtual message that you have sent someone without annoying them, so remember, softly, softly does it. If they haven't responded to you, they may just not be interested, or your message didn't interest them.

I've always admired Seth Godin's work, and when I went to see him present in New York, I knew I was never going to get another chance to say hi. So I did some groundwork several weeks before the event to put myself on his radar. I emailed him directly after reading his book *Poke the Box* and asked him if I could buy him a cup of tea and talk books with him. A very polite 'no' came back and, looking back, I'm sure he gets asked all the time and really, why would he have tea with me? There's nothing in it for him. I didn't pursue it, but I did send him another email some weeks later saying how a particular blog post he had written had resonated with me. He thanked me kindly.

On the day of his presentation in New York, I sat three rows out from the lectern, ready to be inspired by him, with the plan to go backstage straight afterwards to say hello. Unfortunately, he had a very nasty head cold and wasn't feeling too well, and so after his presentation, I respected his privacy and his cold and stayed away. So close!

When I got back home, I came down with a raging cold of my own. Sitting only three rows away from Seth, I must have caught his germs, mustn't I? I wrote a short blog post about my Seth experience and the fact I now had his germs, and posted him the link to it via email and to my surprise and delight, he not only responded back, but he commented on my blog as well.

So nothing came of my planned Seth encounter, but he knows I'm alive, and maybe — just maybe — one day I'll get to shake his hand. That's another plan of mine.

Leveraging

By now you will have had some experience saying hello to someone new every day, making connections with new people and following up where appropriate. Hopefully you've met some wonderful, interesting people along the way, and maybe you've even met them again for a follow-up meeting, done business together or ended up with another business card for your folder. Either way, it's another connection, someone you didn't know even existed yesterday, but now not only have you spoken to them, you may be able to leverage off them too.

Leveraging usually refers to the financial industry where people talk about using one property's value to leverage the value of another when it comes to getting finance, but in the world of meeting new people to gain connections, it's a case of, 'Does this new connection know anyone else who may be of interest to me?'

Remember Tom from chapter 9? He leveraged his blog post on the *Harvard Business Review* site to then get published by *The Economist*. It was this and the fact that his soon-to-be editor at HarperCollins just happened to be opening the morning paper and saw a half-page article written by the same person she had just received a manuscript from. Had Tom not leveraged his *Harvard Business Review* blog article with *The Economist*, he wouldn't have had another article in the national press that morning.

Why do you think some companies advertise the big companies they have worked with in the past on their website and elsewhere? It's to give them credibility and to leverage the respected name for their own gain. We all do it. I have presented to Microsoft in the past, and this is mentioned on my website. I mention it because it allows me a certain amount of credibility with others, particularly on a proposal, and so I use their name and other well-known clients to leverage from to gain other clients.

Name-dropping

I once had a meeting with a lady in PR about an event I wanted to organise called 'The Say Hello Project'. I couldn't create this event on my own; I needed some strategic partners to help me along and in return they would get exposure by association to the event. She liked the idea so I told her my plans about which two other companies I would like to see involved. It just so happened that her husband worked at one of those companies. I could leverage her name when I spoke to him as a way in — a warm call rather than cold-calling him.

Name-dropping is simply leveraging under a different guise, but if you look 'name-dropping' up in a dictionary it has a negative connotation in that people are falsely raising their own standing or credibility to impress others. I just think as long as you don't overdo it and drop names at every single opportunity you can muster, then you're simply using a tool available to you.

Here's an example.

Name-dropping works like a charm

Katrina met the CEO, Rob, of a company she wanted to work for at a taxi rank and started a conversation. He wasn't the person she really needed to talk to about a job in her dream company but, by asking him for the name of the appropriate person, when she did eventually make the call she would undoubtedly drop the CEO's name into the conversation. And why not? She's just spent 10 minutes chatting with him — which she'd certainly also mention during her call.

She found out that the person to call was Carla. When she rang Carla, she said she had been chatting with Rob while they waited for a taxi at the airport and he had passed her name on as the right person to speak with...'

That's leveraging and name-dropping at the same time. Do you think Carla was more receptive to Katrina because she'd been chatting to Rob rather than calling cold? Of course she was.

Leveraging online

What about online connections—people you may not see very often or, in many cases, may have never met. How can you leverage them?

People tend to mix with people similar to them. A-listers tend to mix with other A-listers, royalty with other royalty. So it's pretty obvious that busy executive leaders mix with other busy executive leaders, which is probably not where the majority of other businesspeople hang out. Unless you really get on well with an executive leader or know them personally, it's pretty hard to break into their circle even though you may want to. I liken it to the school disco when my girlfriends and I were young and just starting to notice boys. The boys in the same year as us weren't really of interest to us, but the boys a couple of years older, now that was a different story! The problem was, those boys wouldn't have been seen dead at our year level school disco—it just wasn't cool.

Going back to our executive leaders: they may be more comfortable physically dealing and working with people who they consider a little more 'junior'. But online I have found it a bit different.

The internet can be a great leveller. No-one can see you behind your computer screen and all you have on show is your LinkedIn profile and maybe a presence on a few other sites. You're in control of what people see when they read your profile (and they will) so it has to be a true and accurate reflection of who you are. Don't ever be tempted to lie on any online profile. Liars usually get found out.

Try reaching out to some of your connections online to ask for their help with something, whether you're looking for a new PA or some help getting connected to someone who specialises in raising venture capital. People are usually happy to help and pass on a name or two. Then you can leverage your connection's name again to add credibility to the person you're trying to reach.

Your first message may look like this:

Hi Bill,

Are you able to help?

I am looking to borrow $10 million to cover our expansion plans for the next two years. Do you know of a venture capitalist who could be worth talking to? I would really value any help you could give me.

Many thanks,

John

Short and sweet and to the point.

Hopefully Bill is able to give you a name to get the ball rolling and of course you're going to mention Bill's name when you contact your lead. That immediately gives the receiver of your call a sense of 'Ah yes, I know him well', so it kind of puts everyone at ease and is much less formal than going in cold.

Name-dropping, leveraging—it's all the same thing and, done nicely and genuinely, it turns a cold conversation into a warm one.

~

It really is about making yourself available to the person you're trying to reach, whether it be virtually or in person. Nobody likes to cold call and nobody likes receiving a cold call so any way that you can leverage and name-drop a shared connection and add a little personality into the mix makes the introduction so much easier all round.

Chapter 13
Behavioural profiles

We considered behaving, but it's against our nature.

O.R. Melling

In any business communication, whether it be in person or virtually, it really helps to know what sort of person you're talking to, and by that I mean their behavioural style, which makes up their behavioural profile.

Determining people's behavioural profiles fascinates me and I believe everyone should have a basic understanding of it. Not only can this information give you a better understanding of why you do some of the things *you* do and feel the things *you* feel, but you can understand other people more clearly too. I think it's a great skill to have in business, but also one that anyone living with a partner or family should also understand.

The concept of profiling behaviour was developed in the 1920s by psychologist Dr William Marston, who had a theory that there are four basic personality types, characterised by the following letters: D for Dominance, I for Influence, S for Steadiness and C for Conscientiousness (or DiSC®).

Incidentally, Dr Marston was also credited with developing the first accurate lie detector.

There are many behaviour profiling tools available and they all work on the same principle; they just use different icons or names. One adaptation of DiSC® is BEST (bold-expressive-sympathetic-technical). Another adaptation, Dr Gary Couture's version, uses bird names (dove, owl, peacock and eagle) and others use four different colours, shapes and so on. They're all based on the same four quadrants and they amount to the same four behavioural styles.

My personal favourite behaviour assessment tools are the DiSC® method (www.discprofile.com) and the Extended DISC® System, which you can find at www.extendeddisc .com. They're both great tools and I suggest you test yourself as it's enlightening to see what you find out about yourself.

DiSC® behavioural profiling

DiSC® behavioural profiling is based on four quadrants:

- dominance
- influence
- steadiness
- conscientiousness.

Figure 13.1 shows the four quadrants of the DiSC® behaviour assessment tool.

Figure 13.1: DiSC® profiling

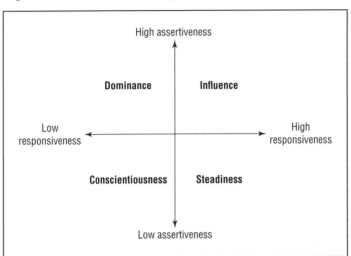

You may see yourself in one of these four quadrants already. Here's some information about each quadrant to give you a more detailed picture of each personality type.

The 'dominance' quadrant mainly describes people who:

- are in a hurry
- are direct and blunt
- will interrupt you
- only need the top-line executive summary
- want to know what the bottom line is for them
- are aggressive and demanding.

If you fall into the 'influence' quadrant you're likely to:

- be open and friendly
- talk a lot
- get excited
- be animated
- talk about others you know
- not be worried about detail
- not listen for a long time.

People in the 'steadiness' quadrant are:

- calm and easygoing
- not usually excitable
- good listeners
- keen to build a relationship before doing business
- good at keeping their opinions to themselves.

'conscientious' people:

- are reserved and quiet
- are detail focused
- ask lots of questions
- are cautious
- look for proof
- study information carefully.

So there you have a very broad brushstroke of what each quadrant's behavioural profile looks like. But most people are not just one or the other; they can be a combination of two or even three of the quadrants. For instance, when I took the test, I found that I was pretty much an equal split between 'I' and 'S'. When I think about the type of person I think I am, influential and steady is spot on. I would hate to think that I had upset someone in some way and I like to build a relationship with the person I'm talking to in order to make more friends and acquaintances.

My husband, on the other hand, is at the opposite end of the behavioural profile diagram: dominant (D), with a large chunk of C (conscientiousness), as attention to detail is important to him. That makes us, as a couple, a pretty good match.

So now you can probably see where in the quadrants you sit.

Try this

You may be able to see immediately where your partner sits on the quadrant. Don't forget they may be a mix of two or three areas and not just one, so it may be better to get in touch with DiSC® and go through the test together. It will help you better understand each other.

Next, you need to assess the behaviour of the people you want to get to know. How should you react to someone you're meeting? How do you relate or 'sell' to another person? Let's look at each quadrant again and see what you can do to make it easier for a new relationship to evolve.

Under each quadrant heading in figure 13.1, we could insert a list of things to do in order to be sympathetic to the natural style of a person whose personality falls in that quadrant, as shown in figure 13.2 (overleaf).

Figure 13.2: how to behave towards people once you have determined their DiSC® behavioural profile

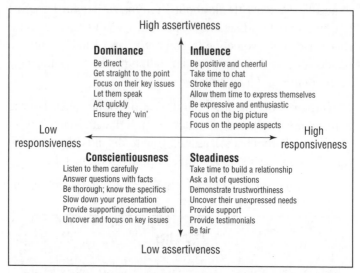

So if, for example, you were talking to someone who is a high D (dominant), you'd need to be direct, focus on the key issues and let them speak. If you were talking to an S (steadiness) person, you'd need to spend some time chatting and building a relationship. If you were to try chatting and building a relationship with a D (dominant) you'd drive them nutty because they would just want you to get on with it!

It's worth pointing out at this stage that you can force yourself to be someone you're not, but it takes a huge amount of energy to be able to carry it off for any length of time. When you come under stress, your natural self will surface—not who you're trying to be.

DiSC® in action: business

I once went to meet with the CEO of a chamber of commerce to talk about running some social media workshops for the members. I was led into the meeting room to wait for him. When he entered, he shook my hand, we sat and he went straight to the point. When he started talking it was obvious what profile he was: he had a chunk of D. A *huge* chunk.

There was absolutely no preamble at all, no chitchat or pleasantries—just straight to it. I was a little unnerved to start with but my radar was turned on so I immediately knew how to react: give him the executive summary, the details, how it will affect his bottom line and tell him when I could begin running the workshops. Bang, bang, bang. I don't think the meeting lasted longer than 10 minutes because he had what he needed to make the right decision. His assistant finalised the deal the following week.

What do you think would have happened if I had insisted on doing things my way, talking chitchat and superfluous nonsense about the lovely weather and what he did at the weekend? I probably would have bored him to tears and maybe missed out on a deal, but because I could read the situation quickly, I could easily adapt my style. I'm the one who had to adapt, not the other way around. On the other hand, if the person I was meeting was just like me, an 'I' and 'S', then we would have been having a great time making small talk about the weekend and where we were going for our holidays, and an hour may have passed before the deal was worked out.

DiSC® in action: personal

When my husband Paul (D and some C) asks me to clean his road bike, I do so because it makes me happy to help (I and S) and not because I'm soft. When I need some help planning for the bigger picture of my business life or making gluten-free bread, he's the man for the job. He'll spend hours on a wet Sunday afternoon following baking recipes to the letter and doing a great job creating wonderful gluten-free baked goods. It's a nice trade-off that works well for both of us.

I also struggle coming up with something different for dinner every night—like lots of people who cook for their family—as our food tends to follow a routine. As we're both fairly health conscious and active, we like to maintain our weight or drop some weight if a cycling event is coming up. Our diet can be a little restrictive in that we don't eat carbohydrates after lunch, and we eat lots of salad vegetables. From my point of view (I and S) I want to provide variety to our meals and ensure that Paul is eating something tasty each night. From Paul's point of view, he couldn't care less what he eats because what I'm currently serving up is a means to an end in keeping his weight down during cycle racing times (D and C). He's not wedded to the process; he's only wedded to the outcome.

Assessing a person's behavioural profile

When you meet someone for the first time, you may not have much to go on to detect their behavioural profile until you hear them speak. So how can you work out their profile type? The short answer is you really can't, unless they're talking to someone else and you're able to observe. If the person is 'holding court' at your local networking event with people gathered around hanging on their every word, you can bet on them being a sociable and influential (I) person. If the person is in a serious conversation with someone else, talking about the details of a current news story, for example, they may well be a conscientious (C) type of person. Once you get to meet a person and speak to them yourself, you may be able to pick up the details you need. Not everyone will be easy to read—certainly those people who are a combination of quadrants won't be—but if someone you come across is mainly one or the other, they should be fairly obvious to

spot. You can find out more information by taking a DiSC®
test yourself.

~

Use the tools that are available to you to build better
relationships with others. By having a basic understanding of
how people you deal with are wired, you have a much better
understanding of what makes them tick. Every partnership in
life and in business should go through the process to maintain
harmony at home and in the workplace.

Disclaimer: I am not personally affiliated with DISC®.

Part summary

You must make a simple plan both for networking in person and online. This really just needs to indicate the general direction in which you wish to go. Make a list of everyone you want to meet in person and everyone you want to meet virtually (for now, even though you may meet them in person in the future). Without your end point, you won't know when you've arrived there. Some people will be on both lists: virtual for now, in person later on, just like my story about trying to meet Seth Godin...one day...!

Leverage wherever you can, both in person and virtually, as name-dropping done the right way will open doors. One thing is certain: if you don't drop names at appropriate times, it will be that much harder for you to get to your end point.

Understanding behavioural profiles is a great skill to have and will certainly put you one step ahead of someone who is not tuned in to what the person they are talking to wants.

Try practising spotting the behavioural profiles of those around you, looking for the main characteristics of each quadrant. Can you spot them in your close family and friends?

Try this

Try behaving according to a behavioural profile that's not naturally you. It can be hard but it's not impossible.

When you next meet someone for the very first time — maybe you have an appointment with them — see how quickly you can pick up on their style and adjust accordingly.

In a nutshell

- Put together a plan for getting to know those people you wish to connect with.

- Make a list of who they are and where you might find them both online and offline.

- Leverage whenever you possibly can. It certainly opens more doors.

- Use behavioural profiles to adjust yourself to what the person you're talking to wants.

Part V

How to boost and utilise your personal network

Starting with hello is good manners, as well as being a strategy for getting a wider connection base, but it need not all be about business. Plenty of people are looking for Mr or Ms Right. You can apply the same strategies we've been using throughout this book to your personal life.

Read the following chapters to learn:

- how to turn acquaintances into friends
- about finding Mr or Ms Right
- how to join a voluntary organisation.

Chapter 14

Networking socially

Friendship is born at that moment when one person says to another: 'What! You too? I thought I was the only one!'

C.S. Lewis

Whatever your belief of where we originated from, people as a whole are sociable creatures; we were put on this earth to pair up, reproduce and build communities. It's our natural role in life so it makes sense to talk about building relationships with others on a more personal level, not just for business.

There have been plenty of relationships forged purely for friendship and even romance, and what tickles me is that we predominantly feel quite happy chatting to strangers when we don't have 'the pressure' of making a business connection on our shoulders but are able to simply be ourselves in a relaxed environment.

Think about the groups of friends you had when you were at school or university and how simple it was to make new friends, particularly as the group of friends you were acquainted with joined forces with others as they came along and in turn introduced their friends, and so on. Your wider friendship network grew steadily and, depending on whether or not you were dating at the time, your friends and acquaintances shifted back and forth as their relationships changed too.

Only this morning as I went to get my morning coffee from the café, a young man who was working on the building site next door chatted easily to me as we waited for our coffee to arrive. No pressure, just friendly banter about the cake I was quickly devouring. I didn't feel like I was being chatted up; he was just being friendly. If I bump into him again, we'll say hi—another person I'm now acquainted with who made for a pleasant morning.

How did you meet your life partner?

Once we have met our life partner, we stop looking—and for good reason. Unless you live in an environment where having multiple partners is acceptable, you're asking for trouble if you don't stop! But think about the process you went through to find your partner: the places you frequented, the chat-up lines you may have used, the number of frogs you had to kiss to find your prince/ss and how much money you probably spent wooing them, all in the name of finding a life partner.

Some people use a dating service. Some will go on blind dates set up by their friends. Some will meet at clubs where there's a common interest and some will meet at their workplace, which is perhaps the most common place for a relationship to flourish. It seems quite a good spot for meeting your future partner is at the supermarket, as the signs of someone who is single are very easy to see by looking at their shopping basket.

The list is endless.

I met my husband at work, and if I hadn't answered a newspaper job advertisement all those years ago (before the internet for sure), I wonder who I may have found as my life partner and how different my life could be now. But I doubt if I could be any happier.

Janette met her husband of 18 years on the ski slopes of Whakapapa in New Zealand, where she lives. I love the idea of the singles queue she refers to.

Janette's story

It's 18 years since my husband and I met in the singles queue on the far west T-bar, skiing at Whakapapa in a blizzard! I was wearing a facemask and he was wearing a balaclava.

We chatted about the usual stuff on the T-bar lift, and then when he skied off I thought 'wow'. He could ski very well. I decided to see if I could keep up, and so we quickly ended up back in the T-bar queue together again.

When we got to the car park at the end of the day and disrobed out of our ski gear, I was quite impressed with what he looked like! Hilariously, when we each removed all our headgear, I thought, 'Oh, he's cute' and, since my headband had been pressed into my forehead by my hood, he thought, 'Oh, she's cute. Shame about those dreadful acne scars.' That night, we caught up at the pub and the following weekend I took him to my law firm ball... and the rest is history!'

Opportunities come to us in all shapes and sizes and in both our business and our personal lives. Think back to how you met the love of your life. How did the story unfold?

Simon's opportunity began with a serendipitous encounter.

Act on that serendipitous moment... or you may never see her again!

Simon met his wife-to-be for the very first time on a pedestrian crossing. He was crossing the road, she was staring at him and he stared back, quite smitten with what he was looking at. He walked on, never expecting to see her again, but the following day, he saw her again with a man who he knew worked at his local bookstore. He decided there and then that he would ask the man about this mystery lady next time he went in.

Two days later, he popped in to find that the man was out of town on a sales trip and standing behind the counter filling in was Simon's wife-to-be. Their relationship blossomed and the rest is history. She did let him in on the fact that the reason she was staring that day on the pedestrian crossing was because she couldn't believe anyone would wear such a hideous jacket. Ouch!

Had Simon not made the effort to go to the bookstore, who knows whether he'd be married now.

Do parents have more friends?

I think it's fair to say that most newly married couples go on to start a family and with that comes a whole new opportunity to meet other people through antenatal classes, playgroup, kindergarten, the school years and so on.

New friends are often made at antenatal classes because you all have something in common—you're all having a baby, you're all excited and you're probably all a bit anxious about the prospect of parenthood too. Prospective first-time parents attend class, chitchat along the way, then possibly start to meet socially as the relationship blossoms, increasing their circle of friends. As time passes and the little one goes on to playgroup, another set of acquaintances is made with some people becoming close friends, and those relationships may go on through kindergarten and throughout the school and college years.

A pattern has formed, one that forms for many people, but not for everyone. If you've never had a family of your own, have you missed out on all of those friends? Does that make you lonely and isolated? Absolutely not. Despite not having had children myself, I certainly don't feel that I've missed out on friends; I just have to make them in other places, places where people without children go.

While chatting outside the school gate with other parents each day was not really an option for me, I have more of my own time to spend going away at weekends to cycling and running events with my husband and competing alongside others with the same interests. Saying hello to a complete stranger while we both wait for our partners to come through the finish line is equally as enjoyable as the school gate conversations, but can you build a lasting friendship with so many casual encounters? Many of the people you see at such events may also frequent other similar events, so you'll often meet them again at another finishing line or even in a coffee shop in the town where the event is being held, as has indeed happened to us many times.

Dave tells his story of a chance meeting on a plane that had a real impact on him and even helped him and his wife with their decision to try for a third child.

Dave's story

Two years ago, one rainy morning in New York, I caught a flight to Boston. My first two scheduled flights were cancelled, and I almost decided not to go, but I gave it one more shot, and the third flight went out as planned. I was sitting in the front row of economy and, just before the flight took off, a much older man got up from first class, which was actually a lot more crowded, and sat down in my row, just across the aisle.

As the plane went into the air, for a short time I couldn't stare at my electronic device of choice, so I peered to my right, and saw the older man reading a paper with large print typed on it. I couldn't help but notice the words on the page: 'My dear friend, the late Ted Kennedy...'

Intrigued, I read on and saw the following words soon thereafter:

'When I wrote the new GI bill...'

I was sitting next to a congressman! Excited, but still not knowing who he was, I put out my hand and said to him, 'Excuse me. Sorry to bother you, but I just wanted to say it's an honour to meet you. I'm Dave Kerpen.'

'Great to meet you, Dave. I'm Senator Frank Lautenberg,' he replied.

We proceeded to talk for the next 45 minutes, the entire flight up to Boston. It turned out that he was on his way to give a speech at his grandson's school. Having nearly run for political office myself, I was anxious to learn from him. I did learn a great deal about the senator: his illustrious career, being the oldest living senator (at 89!), having authored the legislation to ban smoking on airlines—legislation that has affected us all in a positive way. He also authored the *Ryan White CARE Act*, which serves AIDS patients, and fought for stiffer drink-driving penalties. He has had what anyone of any political party would argue is a great career in government and he began it all late in life, having started at the age of 58.

The incredible thing I learned was that before politics Lautenberg had another career in business as the first salesperson and long-time CEO of a payroll company you may have heard of, Automatic Data Processing (ADP). Today, ADP is a 10-billion-dollar company on the Fortune 500. Senator Lautenberg shared stories from its start, in 1949, when he had just graduated from college, and from 1961, when he took the company public.

We talked about business, politics, social media and family. I told him how interested I was in growing my social media business, and then perhaps going into politics, as he had done. I also told him my wife and I were considering having a third child, but we weren't sure because we were both so busy with work and other priorities. It was a great conversation, or at least I thought so. Of course, the flight from New York to Boston had to end. It seemed to me that we had only just taken off and there we were already landing.

Senator Lautenberg gave me his business card, and told me he really enjoyed meeting me and had learned a lot from me about social media. He said he'd love to get together again. I wasn't sure I'd see him again, but I thanked him profusely and told him he'd given me a lot to think about in terms of creating a legacy, as he had done.

'One more thing, Dave,' Senator Lautenberg said, as the flight attendant welcomed us to Boston. 'I want to show you a picture of my greatest legacy.'

As he reached into his pocket, I wondered what he'd show me, a leader so accomplished in two totally different careers. A piece of paper with the idea for ADP? A section of a law he'd written? A picture of him with a president?

Senator Lautenberg pulled his phone out of his pocket and proceeded to show me a picture of himself with a whole bunch of people.

(continued)

Dave's story *(cont'd)*

'These are my four kids and seven grandchildren, Dave. This is my greatest legacy.'

What I learned from that flight

- You can learn from anyone. Start up a conversation whenever possible. Life gives us so many opportunities to strike up a conversation with a stranger—on a flight, waiting in line at the supermarket, or on the train to work, to name a few. We can keep to ourselves, or say hello with a smile when we meet someone, and maybe even learn from them. I learned so much from Frank Lautenberg in just 45 minutes—and the crazy thing is, he actually said he learned from me.

- It's never too early—or too late—to pursue a dream. Frank Lautenberg built one of the largest companies in the world and began when he was just 25. Then he became a US senator at 58 years of age and will have served for more than 30 years. Whatever our dreams are, it's always the right time to go for it.

- Our ultimate, most important legacy is our children. The end of my conversation with Frank Lautenberg had a profound impact on me, and eventually helped my wife and me make the decision to try to have a third child. If a man so accomplished in both business and government could argue that his greatest legacy is his family, how could I not?

I'll close with one more thing Senator Lautenberg shared at the end of our conversation that I think about nearly every day: 'ADP, and the US Senate, won't be on my tombstone. My kids' names all will be.'

Talk about making you think! What a wonderful chance meeting and great story that shows not only the power of that particular chance conversation, but the senator's wisdom too.

I too had a chance encounter while sitting next to someone. I sat next to a man called Charles at a celebratory dinner for the country's top 200 businesses. We chatted for a good deal of the evening about work—he works for a printing and distribution company—and also about sporting activities we had in common, such as cycling and swimming. It was at this point that he mentioned he was going to attempt the harbour swim coming up at the weekend. I was also going to be there supporting a friend, but I thought no more about it.

Heading out of the car park on event day, guess who I bumped into again, this time dressed in a wetsuit? Charles. Had I not met him at that dinner event, we probably would never have noticed each other at the race.

We later connected on LinkedIn. I sent him a brief note to enquire if he had been happy with his time in the swimming race, and he called to thank me and to make a coffee appointment to chat about my business and how I can help him further. Even if it comes to nothing, if I ever have the need or know anyone with the need for volume printing and magazine distribution, I have his details and I can pass his name on.

Join a volunteer organisation

You may belong to an organisation such as Rotary or Lions, which you may have joined with the intention to network with other businesspeople, or to do some good and make new friends outside of the business arena. Many people join for both of these reasons. The type of people at each local branch across the globe will vary, but one thing they all have in common is that they're friendly, welcoming and ready to take you on board to do some good.

Speaking as a Rotarian, although I have only been so for a couple of years, I have met many interesting, lighthearted people, ready to do good work for those in need, as well as a good smattering of corporate and private company heavy hitters. Having lunch sitting next to the CEO of one of the country's top finance institutions, a partner in a big accountancy firm in town or a fellow Rotarian on a student exchange program from another country all add to a relaxed and informal way of acquainting yourself with people from all walks of life and building a solid foundation with them. Next week, I'll be spending one evening packing food parcels with the local Salvation Army for those in need, and I have no idea who I'll meet, but who cares; there will certainly be someone there I haven't met yet and can build a relationship with.

Doing a little good is extremely rewarding, and even more so when you get a thank-you note from the organisation you've helped out.

Try this

Find out about a local Rotary, Lions or similar volunteer group in your area and go along to meet them. You will always receive a welcoming hello from any of these groups.

Conor Cusack tells this amazing story.

Conor's story

The most serendipitous moment of my career was when I was working for a large suburban school district on the northwest side of Rochester in the US. I was employed as a school community partnerships coordinator and was tasked with establishing and sustaining relationships between the school district and various sectors (government, non-profit, health care and business) in and around our county.

One evening I happened to be attending an awards dinner where I had nominated an individual for their positive and outstanding contributions to our students and school district.

It was announced that the University of Rochester was opening the M.K. Gandhi Institute for Nonviolence, a think tank designed to create awareness around the detrimental impact that results from violence.

After dinner I introduced myself to the representatives of the institute and offered my assistance with any projects they may be working on in the near future.

About a week later I received a call from the institute requesting my assistance. The project involved packing and delivering more than 1000 posters of Mahatma Gandhi and his famous messages regarding violence.

I gathered a team of eight high-school student leaders and we accomplished the task, packing the posters into boxes that were delivered to hundreds of schools in our area.

About a month later I received an envelope from the Gandhi Institute. Inside, there was a letter that read:

(continued)

Conor's story *(cont'd)*

Dear Mr Cusack,

For the past 15 years I have lectured around the world and I am happy to say that the youth are eager to find an alternative to violence. I commend you on your work on the Assets and thank you for your enthusiastic response to our outreach into the schools.

Arun Gandhi, grandson of Mahatma Gandhi, September 18, 2007

I was astounded. In my hand was a signed letter from the grandson of perhaps one of the greatest champions for peace the world has ever known.

I will never forget opening the envelope and reading that letter for the first time.

Of course getting a thank-you note is not the reason to do some good for others, but it's a lovely gesture nonetheless.

Turning acquaintances into friends

You have, no doubt, by now made some great connections and acquaintances, some of whom you may want to become friends with. And why not? You don't have to limit yourself to collecting business connections; if there's a spark of possible future friendship there, you must act on it. Here's an example of my own.

Another one of my own stories

I met a man at my local Rotary club called Brian. After we had chatted for a while, I realised he lived not too far away from me and he owned a sizeable piece of land that he farmed. As I live on an orchard, we compared notes about pruning fruit trees as well as talking about what we both did for a living.

We were getting on very well and Brian suggested that my husband and I come to his place one evening for dinner. I assumed at that stage the invitation was just idle chitchat. But a couple of weeks later I saw Brian again, and again he suggested dinner. We exchanged emails and a date was set.

A couple of weeks later we went to Brian's house for an extraordinary meal, to which he had also invited another friend, Mary, who worked at the University Business School. The evening was filled with lively and interesting conversation, great food and lovely wine, and we all had a wonderful time.

I followed up the next day by mailing Brian and his wife a short handwritten note to thank them and to invite them for dinner at our place the following month. The blossoming of a new friendship was slowly taking shape.

Obviously you're not going to be invited to dinner by everyone you meet, but if you think there's a future friendship in the making, do something about it.

When you've met someone you'd like to form a friendship with, look out for:

- a common interest: something that you both enjoy doing
- whether you laugh and joke with each other easily
- whether you really hit it off together.

Sometimes you just pick up a great vibe about someone.

My husband is a keen cyclist. Striking up a conversation with the man sitting next to him on a recent flight, he discovered that the man, Barry, was also hooked on riding bikes. Not only that, but they lived only 15 minutes away from each other. After sharing the journey home together, they organised to go out riding together at the weekend. They are both in business, so what started out as being a pleasant chat could mean future business connections as well as a new cycling buddy.

Recently, I needed some out-of-the-box thinking for a project I was working on for a client, and I really didn't have a clue where to find the information I needed. Google wasn't any help in this instance, so I reached out to a bunch of total strangers on LinkedIn and sent them each a message through the paid premium account, InMail.

One lady, Barbara, came back with an offer to help. She sent an email around to connections she thought could be useful to me and copied me in. Not much happened from there, but she came back to me later on to find out if I'd received any response. I replied, 'Not much, but thanks for trying. Looks like I'm on my own with this one.' Because she didn't want to see me struggle with it, she suggested that we arrange to meet up and discuss the project in more detail. As she lived about fours hours away by car, she said she would let me know when she was next coming my way.

Two weeks later, she came. I met her for a coffee and ran through my project again. Not only was she extremely helpful and very generous with her time, she also knew exactly who I needed to be put in contact with and promised to arrange this. You know how sometimes you get the feeling, 'Wow, what a nice person. Aren't they just awesome?' That was Barbara. The conversation was easy, we had some things in common and I'm sure I'll be seeing her again. The thing to do next time is to make the effort to nurture the beginnings of a friendship too—take some positive action and see what happens.

Get out on the golf course

So what about other social pastimes? Have you ever wondered what a game of golf can teach you about people? Quite a lot, when you know what to look for.

It's common knowledge that many relationships are forged and deals are won on the golf course, and I always thought it was because the sport appealed to rich people who can afford it. But there are many more sporting activities that are far more costly than golf, such as car racing, yachting and horse racing. So what makes golf so special when it comes to firming relationships and closing deals?

It turns out that it's really nothing to do with the expense of the sport, but the amount of time you get to spend with the other players and what you can observe during that time. When you're out of your normal work surroundings, you tend to drop your guard, you behave a little differently and you relax a little. Well, so do the others.

Over the four or five hours it takes to hit a round of golf, there are a whole bunch of little giveaways that you can observe about your playing partners. Beware, though: it works both ways. Other players may be watching you, if they're smart enough.

Here are some things to observe:

- Do they move the ball, perhaps when they're in the rough or behind a tree?

- Do some of the players extend the truth a little when it comes to their handicap?

- Do they play out of turn or sequence?

- Do they blame the course, their irons, or the weather for their poor performance?

- Do they criticise other players in jest, laughing it off as they go?

Actually building the relationship is the most important aspect of having a game of golf with a new connection. It's not about showing off and getting the highest score or acting the fool. So be remembered for the right reasons, but have some fun doing it.

Try this

Who do you get on well with at the moment and would like to get to know a little better? Invite them for dinner or for a game of golf. It could be the start of a lovely friendship.

~

Turning colleagues and business acquaintances into friends is an ideal way to get to know them better and develop a deeper connection. Getting together in a social setting allows everyone to drop their guard a little and for people's real personalities to surface. Friends are a great asset to have around.

Chapter 15

Mind your manners

The hardest job kids face today is learning good manners without seeing any.

Fred Astaire

Are you naturally good mannered, and could your good manners help you overcome being a little shy when talking with a stranger?

My husband is a great guy, but he can be a little shy when it comes to meeting people for the first time. He prefers to wait for the conversation to get going and watch people in action before he adds anything into the mix. So I wondered how he approaches strangers in his busy working day. Does he make the effort to talk to them at all or does he simply ignore them? His response at first surprised me, but then when I had thought about it, I was surprised that I was the one who was surprised by his answer because he said, 'It's just good manners to say good morning when you share an elevator with someone, whether you know them or not.'

There you have it: it's just good manners and nothing more, nothing to be scared of, and nothing to avoid; simply good manners. He certainly didn't view saying good morning as a way to grow his business connection base in the elevator going up to his office each day. It was just a natural politeness.

'Please' and 'thank you' go a long way in most cultures and I think that as we seem to be always playing with our smart phone or something else, we use these pieces of equipment as a stopgap, something to fiddle with at awkward moments, rather than using good manners. We seem to always be trying to squeeze another task into our lives whenever we can—such as clearing some emails or tweets—to lighten our digital load.

It can be so easy to forget our manners, as John found out.

Remember your manners

John's wife made a statement to him when they were on holidays. John asked his wife to pass him something without saying please, to which she exclaimed, 'Do you know that these past few months while you've been bogged down with work, you've forgotten to say please when you want something, and it's just struck me that you don't say it at all anymore?'

John hadn't even realised that he wasn't using his manners. He wasn't being deliberately rude. It was just that with being under stress at work, something had to give and unfortunately it was some of his manners. His wife calling him on it and pointing it out was the kick in the backside he needed to start using 'please' again.

So what do you do when you've opened a door for yourself to walk through? Do you walk straight through, letting the door swing back into its frame without a moment's thought for anyone behind you, or do you look behind you first and say 'after you' to the person waiting and then hold the door wide for them as they go through? Incidentally, you don't have to be male to do this. It's one of my pet hates when someone leaves the door swinging in my face without seeing if there's someone else wanting to enter or leave through it. Don't forget to thank the person holding it open for you. Your good manners reflect on your character. You just never know whose face you're letting that door swing into—it could very well be the person you're on your way to meet for the first time!

Here are some other things to think about in relation to manners that may have slipped a little in our fast-paced world.

- *Greet people.* Say hello more often, whether it's the mailman or the barista making your coffee. Just say hello when you come into contact with another person.

- *Speak politely.* Never talk over someone and interrupt them just because you're busting to say something that fits the conversation. Wait and slip it in when you can.

- *Congratulate others on their success.* Whether it's a member of an opposing team, or a colleague who has just had a promotion, congratulate them and be genuine about it.

- *Drive nicely.* It can be hard to do, but is it such a big deal to let someone into your lane ahead of you? Will it slow you down that much? Since I drive a company sign-written car, I really have to watch my 'driving language' because my brand is always on show.

- *Introduce others into the conversation.* Don't let people be wallflowers on the edge. Introduce them to the others in your group and briefly tell them what you've been talking about so they can get up to speed quickly.

- *Be authentic with your manners.* You don't have to be stiff and stuffy, but polish your old manners up and insert them where needed.

- *Don't smoke in front of non-smokers.* Smoking in front of others is not as common as it once was, so you may want to check on etiquette by asking if you may smoke, or leave it until later.

- *Don't arrive late or not at all without calling ahead.* As I'm writing this, I'm waiting for someone to show up who was due over an hour ago. I've received no word that they're going to be held up. Everyone's time is important and, again, it reflects back on your character.

Turn on a smile

It's worth looking at smiling while we're talking about manners because I think they can go hand in hand—pleasant person, pleasant manners. Louis Armstrong famously sang that when you smile, the whole world smiles with you. Have you ever been able to resist smiling when someone smiles right at you? It's pretty hard not to smile, and if you were out in a public area and a complete stranger smiled your way, you'd probably even check behind you because you'd assume they're smiling at someone else. But if they were smiling at you, what would you do? Smile back, even if only in a small way.

Receiving a smile will immediately give you the impression that the person giving the smile is pleasant, open and welcoming. Or perhaps they're paying you a compliment. Whatever it may be, it makes you feel good. Smiling also triggers activity in your brain, in the left frontal cortex to be exact, which is the area that registers happiness. The feel-good effect that comes from our brain sending out a message to let the endorphins out into your bloodstream makes us feel great. Apart from the great feeling a smile gives you, it has also been proven that smiling reduces stress and possibly even blood pressure, so it's definitely up there on the list of things to do daily for a positive mood and good health.

Smiling is one way to get noticed when you're prospecting for new connections and, as most people will smile right back at you, it could be a successful way for you to break into conversation. I would just add a word of warning here though, particularly for women. Smiling at the same sex as yourself is okay, but do be careful when you give a smile to the opposite sex. Unless you're looking for a new life partner, don't overdo it in case they get the wrong idea and chat you up rather than making small talk for business purposes.

Equally, men tend to only smile at other males they already know, maybe out of feeling uncomfortable doing so with a total stranger. It's not surprising then to learn that women are deemed the more social of the two sexes in general.

I had cause to smile at myself recently. I was wearing a rather 'floaty' black-and-white polka-dot dress that had a full circle skirt to it and no matter what mood I am in when I put it on I always feel lighthearted and feminine. I attended an appointment, where the woman I was meeting with complimented me on how stylish my dress looked (I really must wear it more often). The meeting went well, and as I exited the building onto the street below and was standing outside the coffee shop, a gust of wind caught the skirt of my dress and blew it up into the air 'Marilyn Monroe' style! So standing there, right outside the coffee shop, trying to tame my skirt, which was billowing in all directions, all I could do was smile as wildly as my skirt was behaving. It felt good though, so I didn't spoil the mood by looking into the coffee shop to see if anyone had seen my display. That would have been too embarrassing!

As with lots of areas in this book, there isn't much that you don't already know. It's putting all of this into use that makes a difference to your relationships, whether it is with someone you know and you're building a relationship with, or not.

Sometimes, things just happen

Sometimes the people we meet in life help us in ways that we don't realise until later on when something happens. Kim shares her story of how a chance meeting with a yoga teacher and a lucky 'mistake' by her airline probably saved her life.

Kim's story

In 1996 I left my job, unable to work due to chronic fatigue syndrome. I walked in to work one day and quit on the spot, unable to cope with the simplest of tasks. For the next five years I visited more than a hundred natural therapists, seeking answers to this seemingly baffling condition, which no doctor had any answers for. Nothing seemed to work.

Finally one day, while lying in bed with yet another bout of intense fatigue, I asked myself, 'What would you do if you only had six months to live?' I really was beginning to think I was just not meant to live. And the answer came to me: I would do my dream trip around the world. 'So what's stopping you?' was the next question. Well, nothing, apart from exhaustion, and since it seemed I had nothing to lose, why not do it? And the decision was made.

I put my house on the market and it sold to the first couple who walked in the door a week later. I sat down to plan my trip, which started in Hawaii, moved through the US and on to the UK and Europe. Fortunately, due to the fact I had a first-class ticket I was able to alter my itinerary as I liked, and somewhere along the line I re-routed from Canada to the US. Unbeknown to me, this was to be of huge significance.

As the trip progressed, I realised that despite on the one hand still wondering if I might die, another part of me was quite obviously still looking to live. I found my way to a multitude of healers and experienced all sorts of healing phenomena, from sacred sound rituals in Egyptian pyramids to remote tipis and monasteries in the Arizona Desert and a week-long Indian 'Panchakarma' cleansing retreat in Colorado.

On my way back to New Zealand via the US, I travelled to Central America, where I sought out more healers, and experienced shamans cracking eggs over my head in Guatemala and purification sweat lodges (*Temezcal*) in Mexico.

The plan was to visit South America, but an intense bout of fatigue, along with a strong intuition saying it didn't feel right, found me exhausted and stranded in Costa Rica. Unable to move, I rented a tiny apartment in San Jose and awaited my next move.

While there, I discovered a yoga class, and the teacher—newly arrived from the US—mentioned she taught an abdominal massage technique, which is part of the art of Qigong, called 'Chi Nei Tsang' (CNT). I have no idea why, but I was immediately intrigued. I couldn't wait for the class to finish to find out more. She said she could offer me a session, but then said she felt I was too ill to treat, and instead gave me the name of her teacher in San Francisco. She also mentioned that an extraordinary spiritual guru would be visiting Dallas soon, and if I could I should definitely check her out.

I intuitively knew this was the next—and last—leg of my journey before returning to New Zealand. I had one more month left of my 12-month, round-the-world ticket. I set off for Dallas and in the meantime emailed the CNT teacher in San Francisco. It just happened she had a workshop coming up that weekend, and I enrolled on the spot.

I arrived in San Francisco and made it to the workshop. I was immediately fascinated with this unusual massage technique. I asked the teacher how I could find out more, and she gave me the name of her teacher, also in San Francisco. I phoned his office, and was advised he was booked out for two months, but that I could pick up some information. So I made a time to do that.

(continued)

Kim's story *(cont'd)*

Too exhausted to take the train, I arrived at his office in a taxi, and he asked how I was feeling. I immediately burst into tears. Six years of searching, thousands of dollars seemingly down the drain, and it appeared I was no closer to finding a solution. The extraordinary thing was, for some strange reason, despite being booked out two months in advance, he was available. And I remember his exact words: 'I'll give you a little treatment'. That was an understatement.

As I lay on the table receiving my first ever Chi Nei Tsang, he told me, 'The good news is you're strong. The bad news is you're using that strength to hold everything in'. And a floodgate opened. I bawled my eyes out for an hour as he and his assistant worked on me. By the end of the session, although it's hard to describe, it felt like I had been given a completely new belly and I felt like a totally different person. Words can't describe the gratitude and relief I felt. Finally, after six years, I had discovered the cause of my fatigue: emotional suppression.

As I was leaving his office, I noticed a flyer advertising his upcoming CNT training due to start two weeks later and took a copy with me. I travelled back to the hotel by train—so different was my energy from two hours earlier. Back in my hotel room, I read the flyer and just knew I had to do this training. But how? My 12-month ticket was due to expire in two weeks, just when the training was due to start.

I rang the airline, and was adamantly told I could not extend my ticket. I rang my travel agent back home who concurred. I kid you not when I say I sat and looked at my ticket every day for a week, wondering how I could change my flight and make this happen. I just didn't want to lose my first-class ticket back home!

Some strange force kept drawing me to look at the ticket. On about the seventh day, I was holding it in my hand and suddenly noticed the expiry date was incorrect! It should have said 6 July, and it said 6 October! I couldn't believe my eyes. When I had rerouted six months earlier, they had put the wrong expiration date on the reissued ticket!

I immediately phoned my travel agent in New Zealand and asked him if he thought I could 'get away with it'. He said, in theory, yes. So I decided to risk it and stay on for the training. It was a life-changing experience in many ways, both for my own recovery and for my ability, as it turned out later, to help others do so too.

Two months later as I checked in for my flight home, I was terrified I would be found out. I couldn't wait for the flight to take off because surely once in the air they wouldn't turn the plane round!

I returned to New Zealand to continue my recovery, which took another few years and included several trips back to the US to take my Qigong training to practitioner level. Several years ago I started working as a specialist in chronic fatigue and other chronic health conditions, and there is no doubt this would not have happened if I had not attended that very first training. It was the key to my recovery.

How on earth could I have known that a seemingly innocuous mistake made by a ticketing agent six months into my trip would become such a critical piece in the jigsaw puzzle of life several months later? Who knows…but I do feel that somehow it was meant to happen, and I'm forever grateful!

It's amazing where journeys sometimes take you, who you meet along the way and how much those people can change your life, as happened to Dave (from chapter 14) and Kim. How very different their lives might be now.

Part summary

Saying hello isn't just about business; it's about building relationships with all kinds of people who come into your life in some way, whether you're looking for a new business partner or a lifelong love partner. We were born to be sociable creatures, to meet our mates, live in communities and reproduce, so why should it be any different for a business relationship (obviously without the reproduction part!)?

If you're looking for your life partner, you should follow the same principles we've discussed in this book: put yourself in the situation, find the commonality and start with hello — just like Janette did on the ski slopes of New Zealand.

Having children definitely gives you access to a group of people you may not have otherwise met, with the natural flow of events that come with having a child such as antenatal classes and then school. Even if you don't have children, there are still many places where you can meet others, particularly if you have something in common. You just need to seek them out and show up.

Try this

Is there someone you really get on with in a professional manner and you'd like to be friends with? Why not invite them to dinner, and perhaps ask another party or two at the same time? If you don't make the effort to turn a particular business relationship into a friendship as well, it may never happen.

If you still feel a little shy about approaching someone you don't know yet, simply think of it as good manners. For example, it's good manners to say hello when you're sharing an elevator with someone. You don't have to have an agenda to say hello.

In a nutshell

- We were born to be sociable creatures and live in communities with others. That's our natural role.

- If you're looking for love or friendship, the same principles in this book apply.

- Find places such as sports clubs where you can make more friends.

- Make a conscious effort to turn a good business relationship into a friendship where appropriate.

- Remember, it's simply good manners to start with hello.

Conclusion

Whatever your reason for wanting to expand your connection and/or friendship base, it's not that hard if you know where to start, what to look out for and how to follow it up. You have the knowledge now to go forth and connect and I really hope you do that. Let me know about your stories whenever something good comes from your endeavours. I'd love to hear them. And, who knows, you may find them in a follow-up book in the future.

I sincerely hope this book has been useful to you and has given you the confidence to say, 'Yes, it can be easy to meet strangers—they're simply people you don't know yet, and it all starts with hello.'

Linda Coles

Index

Why not share the content in this book with your team, **presented directly from the author?**

...or choose

Start with Hello
How to convert today's stranger into tomorrow's client.

Ever wondered why some businesspeople have all the luck? They talk to more people!

It's not about being lucky; it's about talking to more people, more of the time and you can only do that by starting with hello.

New conversations and new connections will lead to new opportunities, you just need to be open to the idea of talking to complete strangers and act on the signs you receive to make an opportunity happen.

Life Online
Mastering the online social platforms made easy!

With humour and real life stories, your audience will have no trouble understanding what they have to do next to increase their online brand and how to do it.

Immediately empower them to use the social media online tools to improve their brand awareness online and ultimately their bottom line.

Contact me:
linda@bluebanana20.com
bluebanana20.com

Get a great content driven, light bulb moment presenter for your next event and your team will love you forever!

Learn more with practical advice from our experts

microDomination
Trevor Young

The Ultimate Book of Influence
Chris Helder

Power Stories
Valerie Khoo

The New Rules of Management
Peter Cook

Outlaw
Trent Leyshan

Hooked
Gabrielle Dolan and Yamini Naidu

How to Present
Michelle Bowden

Play a Bigger Game
Rowdy McLean

Think Write Grow
Grant Butler

Available in print and e-book formats WILEY